TIMESAVER FOR EXAI

Writing

FOR FIRST (FCE)

By Fiona Davis

Contents

Introduction

Who is this book for?

This book is for teachers of students who are preparing for the Writing test in the *Cambridge English: First* or *Cambridge English: First for Schools* exam and who require extra practice material. Ideal as a supplement to any *First* or upper-intermediate coursebook, the topics and activities are especially designed to appeal to older teenage and young adult classes. This resource is also suitable for use with any upper-intermediate classes who wish to develop their writing skills and broaden their vocabulary at B2 level.

The *Cambridge English: First* exam – an overview

Cambridge English: First is a qualification at upper-intermediate level (Level B2 on the CEFR scale) which is officially recognised by universities, employers and governments around the world. The exam is aimed at learners who want to use English for study at an upper-intermediate level, start working in an English-speaking environment or live independently in an English-speaking country.

The *Cambridge English: First for Schools* exam is a version of the *Cambridge English: First* exam which follows the same format and is at the same level. The *Cambridge English: First for Schools* exam contains content and topics which are especially appropriate for school-age learners.

The exam consists of four tests: Reading and Use of English, Writing, Listening, and Speaking. Students will be given one hour and twenty minutes to do the Writing test, which is divided into two parts. Part 1 is a compulsory discursive essay. In Part 2, students can choose from three (or four in the *For Schools* exam) different task types. (See the table below.) They are asked to write between 140 and 190 words for each task.

How does this book help your exam students?

The *First* Writing test is challenging. It requires students not only to produce accurate grammar and spelling, but also demonstrate good writing skills: an awareness of the target reader, purpose of the task and the register appropriate to the context.

Exam task answers in the *First* Writing test are assessed in terms of their content, communicative achievement, organisation and language.

Content

The *First* exam requires students to read and understand a task and respond with relevant content. The activities in this Timesaver ask students to read exam tasks carefully and consider what information is required. Each activity is based on a topic which commonly features in the exam and students are given the chance to broaden their knowledge of topic vocabulary and common opinions, as well as brainstorm their own ideas. In the test students' opinions will not be assessed, only how these opinions are expressed.

PART	TASK TYPE	
1	Discursive essay	Students are asked to write a discursive essay in a neutral or formal style. Students read a question or statement and are then asked to give their views on it. Students write about three main ideas, two of which are given as prompts and one idea of their own.
2	Article	This is usually written for an English-language magazine or website. Students should aim to interest and engage the reader who will usually be of a similar age.
3	Email or letter	Students read an extract from an email or letter and write a reply. The response should be in a style appropriate to the situation and recipient.
4	Review	Usually written for an English-language magazine or website. In the review, students can express their personal opinion of something they have experienced, e.g. a book, a holiday or a product.
5	Report	Candidates make suggestions or recommendations for a superior (e.g. their boss) or their peer group
6	Story	The story appears in the *First for Schools* exam only. Students are given the first sentence and two prompts to include in the story.
7	Set text	This is an optional activity in the *First for Schools* exam only. Students can discuss features of a set text or the film version of it.

Communicative achievement

This covers how appropriate the writing is for the task. Students should not include informal language in formal correspondence, but equally they need to avoid formal language in a task type such as an article or review for an English-language website. This Timesaver has a number of activities focussing on formal and informal register, as well as the more neutral style common in emails. Students are asked to consider who they are writing for and the functional language that is required. Examples of functions covered in the activities are: comparing and contrasting, giving advice, making suggestions and recommendations, giving reasons, reporting feedback, generalising, and in emails: apologising and accepting or rejecting an invitation. Useful Language lists are included to signpost this language to students. Any of the task types might include such functional language as part of the task.

Organisation

Students should aim to develop a clear and logical writing style. Many of the activities in this Timesaver ask students to think about how their work is organised: making use of cohesive devices and linkers. Students are encouraged to make notes and plan their work, making good use of paragraphs to express their ideas clearly. How to approach writing an introduction is discussed, as is writing a convincing conclusion. Students are given advice in coming up with ideas for the articles and story tasks.

Students have two questions to answer in one hour and twenty minutes which works out at forty minutes per question. They should aim to spend the first ten minutes of this time thinking of and organising their ideas and also leave themselves five minutes at the end of the task to read through their work. Reading through your work is an essential part of good writing and activities are provided which help students to practise this. Even with time allowed for planning and checking, this still leaves twenty-five minutes actual writing time which the average student should find adequate for the number of words required.

Make sure you give students adequate practice of writing under timed conditions so that they are confident in writing to task and within the wordcount. Students who write noticeably more than the recommended wordcount may find that the final part of their essay is not marked. However, students who write noticeably under the wordcount will probably not have included all the content required.

Language

Students will be marked on the accuracy of their language but also the range and complexity of the language attempted. The activities in this Timesaver give lots of opportunity for vocabulary development, enabling students to make the appropriate topic word choice as well as encouraging them to 'show off' their knowledge of English.

How do I use this book?

This book consists of 30 stand-alone photocopiable lessons, as well as two complete practice tests. The lessons can be used in any order, require little preparation and are suitable for supplementing main coursebooks. Each lesson includes a clearly signposted **EXAM TASK**, tips on how to approach exam tasks, and a variety of activities to use before and after the main writing task.

- The activities are designed to be teacher-led, but are used without separate Teacher's notes. Clear instructions are on the pages, which are all photocopiable.

- The task type and focus are clearly labelled at the top of each lesson.

- The lessons are designed to last approximately one hour, not including the time needed for writing the **EXAM TASK**. Please note that timings may vary according to class size, level of language, etc.

- Where appropriate, students are asked to work in pairs or small groups to generate more language and engage students more fully in the tasks.

- The comprehensive answer key at the back of the book provides an explanation of the answers. Sample answers are provided for the exam practice tasks. These are a rich resource of language which can also be exploited for classroom use. Students can find examples of useful phrases in these and/or compare register and content with their own work. They are also a good basis for classroom activities, such as wall dictations or gap-fills.

We hope these activities help to increase your students' confidence in written English and that they will add to your students' enjoyment of learning English for the *Cambridge English: First* exam.

The Timesaver series

The Timesaver series provides hundreds of ready-made lessons for all levels, topics and age groups. Other *Timesaver for Exams* titles are available for the Listening and Reading and Use of English exams. Check out these and other Timesaver titles at **www.scholastic.co.uk/elt**.

Great work

1 Work in pairs. Match the people to the quotes. Do you agree with these points of view?

Serena Williams,
tennis player

Marlon Brando,
actor

Steve Jobs,
entrepreneur

Oscar Wilde,
author

Michelle Obama,
lawyer

1

"Never confuse the size
of your paycheck with
the size of your talent."

2

"When I was young
I thought money was the most
important thing in life; now that I
am old I know that it is."

3

"Everyone's dream can come true, if
you just stick to it and work hard."

4

"The only way to do
great work is to love
what you do."

5

"Success isn't about how much money
you make. It's about the difference you
make in people's lives."

2 Brainstorm as many jobs as you can for each category. Discuss with a partner. Do you have similar choices?

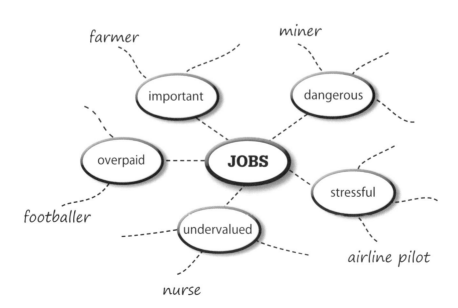

PHOTOCOPIABLE

3 Complete the sentences to summarise some of your discussion in exercise 2.

a) In my country, being a .... is well-respected. As a result ....

....

b) In my opinion, ... are undervalued. It must be ....

4 Write headings for each group of phrases. Which of these phrases have you used in today's lesson?

1 ....

In my opinion …

For me …

I think …

I believe …

From my point of view …

To my mind …

In my view …

As far as I am concerned …

2 ....

This is because …

One reason for this is …

It must / can be (difficult) to …

This has the effect of *(+verb+-ing)* …

As a result …

Exam tip!

Always give reasons for your opinions.

5 Read the exam task and write your essay in 140–190 words. Use phrases from exercise 4.

 **EXAM TASK**

In your English class you have been talking about jobs and salary. Now, your teacher has asked you to write an essay.

Write your essay using **all** the notes and giving reasons for your point of view.

Professional sportspeople deserve the high salaries they earn. Do you agree?

Notes

Write about:

1. training

2. social equality

3. .... (your own idea)

Transport going forward

1 You are going to read about environmentally-friendly forms of transport for cities in the future. These phrases from the articles are not complete. Before you read, work in pairs to guess what they are.

a) traffic ....

b) urban ....

c) .... of transport

d) rush ....

e) cycle ....

f) fossil ....

g) rechargeable ....

h) .... emissions

2 Read the texts. Were your guesses correct?

Cycling

In urban areas, the fastest and most efficient way of getting around is often by bicycle. The average speed of cars in Mexico City, for example, is 4 kph in the rush hour, while bicycles average 10 kph. But cycling in a city can be dangerous. No bike helmet will protect you from a careless driver of a lorry. In the Danish city of Copenhagen, however, one-third of all commuters get to work by bike. There are 350 km of cycle paths which are raised from the road and safe to cycle on.

....

Self-driving cars

Google engineers in the USA have already started testing self-driving cars on the roads. By using a combination of lasers, radars and GPS, the cars can analyse information about their surroundings faster than a human can. Even taking into account the risk of the car computer malfunctioning, self-driving cars could make transport safer by eliminating the cause of 95 per cent of today's accidents: human error. Some experts believe we'll see this new means of transport on the market by 2025, but self-driving cars are likely to be very expensive.

Eco-friendly cars

Electric cars are a great step forward in the race to find alternatives to fossil fuels and cut down on pollution. The electric vehicle (or EV) gets its power from rechargeable batteries. No need to buy petrol and no need to feel guilty about carbon emissions or noise pollution. However, electric charging points are still new and are not found in many places. If you run out of charge, you're going nowhere. Charging your car at home is convenient, but it could leave you with a high electricity bill.

....

SkyTran

SkyTran is a system of high-speed commuter pods which is being considered in places as diverse as Tel Aviv in Israel, Toulouse in France and Kerala in India. SkyTran uses the power of electromagnets to float above guide rails. This cuts down on friction, allowing much quicker and quieter travel than on conventional trains. SkyTran will produce zero emissions and operate above the city, avoiding traffic congestion. The main disadvantage is the cost of the infrastructure. SkyTran could cost as much as $10 million per mile to construct.

3 **Look at the adjectives below. In pairs, discuss which forms of transport you think they describe.**

a) eco-friendly   c) dangerous   e) efficient

b) high-speed   d) quiet   f) expensive

4 **Look at this essay exam task and answer the question below.**

> Is cycling the best form of transport for the future?
>
> Write about:
>
> 1. the environment
>
> 2. fitness
>
> 3. .... (your own idea)

Why is the examiner asking this question?

a) Cycling is a popular form of transport and the examiner wants us to discuss why this is.

b) The examiner wants us to discuss eco-friendly transport solutions, such as cycling.

5 **Which of these is the best introduction to the exam task? Why?**

> **Exam tip!**
>
> *When you write an introduction, show that you have a good awareness of why the examiner is asking this question.*

a *When considering forms of transport, we also need to think about their effect on the environment. Cycling certainly does little damage to the environment, but it may not be suitable for everyone.*

b *Cycling is a slow form of transport which is only suited to young people and fine weather. When thinking about future forms of transport, we should be looking at other more practical forms of transport.*

6 **Read the exam task and write your essay.**

✏ EXAM TASK

In your English class you have been talking about environmentally-friendly forms of transport. Now your teacher has asked you to write an essay.

Write your essay using **all** the notes and giving reasons for your point of view.

Are electric cars the best form of transport for the future?

Notes

Write about:

1. pollution

2. noise

3. .... (your own idea)

A meat-free future

1   **Read this extract from a sample exam answer. What question do you think it is answering?**

As the world population continues to increase and there are more and more mouths to feed, the issue of how we feed the world becomes ever more serious.

There are many who say that a meat-free diet is the only healthy diet. But I would have to disagree. Although there are many health risks associated with eating red meat, such as high blood pressure and heart disease, these are usually symptoms of eating too much meat. In moderation and as part of a balanced diet, red meat is not necessarily a health risk.

In my opinion, the main problem with eating meat is how it is produced. A large proportion of the food we grow today is feed for animals and this is likely to increase. There is not enough land available without cutting down precious habitats like tropical rainforests. Furthermore, there are also water shortages in many parts of the world, which means there is insufficient water to be used in food production.

2   **Look at these people's opinions. Which opinions does the writer mention in the essay? Which opinions do you agree with?**

a Look at the figures. 40% of the food farmed in the world today is for animals. By 2050 the world population will be 9 billion, so this can only increase. There is not enough land or water available to produce this food. Being a vegetarian is not a choice, it's the future.

b Did you know that one of the most harmful of greenhouse gases is methane? It's produced by burning fossil fuels but also by intensive livestock farming. So meat production contributes to pollution.

c I don't know how people get by without eating meat. Vegetables just don't fill me up. Meat has lots of protein and that's what stops you from feeling hungry.

d Eating meat has been associated with lots of health risks such as heart attacks, diabetes and high blood pressure. People are not always aware of all the preservatives that are added to meat. As a vegetarian, I know what's in my food and most of that is vitamins.

e Some people eat less meat for ethical or health reasons, but I think it's about moderation. A little meat is part of a well-balanced diet. It contains iron and zinc that can be difficult to obtain from vegetarian diets.

3   **Match the definitions with the words in the text.**

   a) not having too much of anything

   b) a serious illness caused by too much sugar in the blood

   c) chemicals which make food stay fresh longer

   d) farm animals

   e) concerned with what is right or wrong

   f) a food group which includes meat, eggs, dairy products and nuts

4 Which is the best conclusion for the sample answer? Why?

a) We will not have enough resources to produce all the meat that a growing world population requires and what's more, a meat-free diet is healthier. To conclude, a meat-free diet is the only option for the future.

b) In my opinion, a meat-free diet isn't the only option for the future, but a more balanced diet is. We need to cut down on how much we consume so that there is enough for everyone. What's more, we need to start doing this now.

c) For all these reasons, I firmly believe that a meat-free diet isn't the only option for the future, but a more balanced diet is. We definitely need to include more vegetables in our diet as research shows they are very good for your health.

> **Exam tip!**
>
> *Don't include new arguments or ideas in your conclusion.*

5a Underline one phrase in each of the paragraphs in exercise 4 which is particularly useful in a conclusion.

5b Replace each underlined phrase with one of the phrases below. Which do you prefer?

a) *In conclusion …*   d) *On balance …*

b) *To summarise …*   e) *All in all …*

c) *To sum up …*   f) *As far as I'm concerned …*

6 Work in pairs. Read the exam task and write your essay in 140–190 words.

 EXAM TASK

In your English class you have been talking about vegetarianism. Now your teacher has asked you to write an essay.

Write your essay using **all** the notes and giving reasons for your point of view.

In today's world, we should all be considering a meat-free diet. Do you agree?

Notes

Write about:

1. health

2. pollution

3. .... (your own idea)

7 Swap your essay with another pair and answer these questions.

a) Do the writers agree with the statement?

b) Do the writers include the points of health and pollution in the essay?

c) What other idea did the writers include?

Too young for Facebook?

1 **Read Rose's request for help on an online forum. In pairs discuss what Rose should do.**

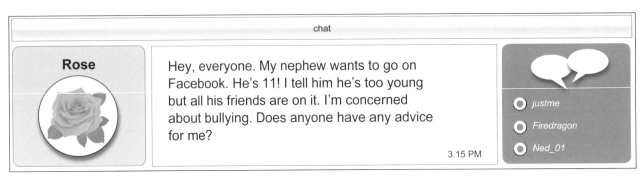

chat

Rose

Hey, everyone. My nephew wants to go on Facebook. He's 11! I tell him he's too young but all his friends are on it. I'm concerned about bullying. Does anyone have any advice for me?

3.15 PM

- justme
- Firedragon
- Ned_01

2 **Read the chatroom posts in reply to Rose. Are any of them similar to your views?**

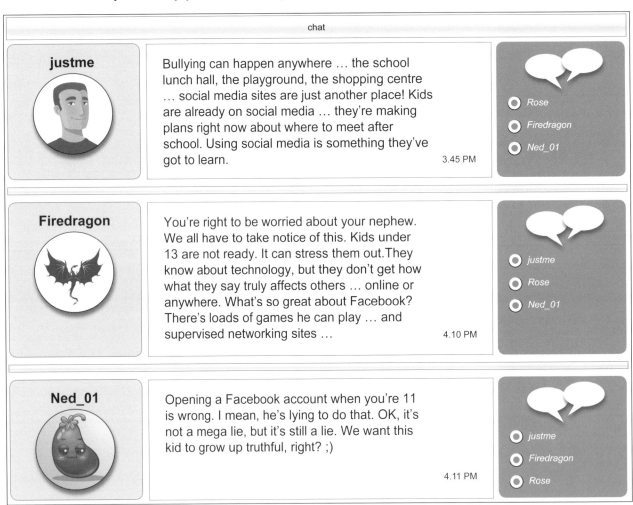

chat

justme

Bullying can happen anywhere … the school lunch hall, the playground, the shopping centre … social media sites are just another place! Kids are already on social media … they're making plans right now about where to meet after school. Using social media is something they've got to learn.

3.45 PM

- Rose
- Firedragon
- Ned_01

Firedragon

You're right to be worried about your nephew. We all have to take notice of this. Kids under 13 are not ready. It can stress them out. They know about technology, but they don't get how what they say truly affects others … online or anywhere. What's so great about Facebook? There's loads of games he can play … and supervised networking sites …

4.10 PM

- justme
- Rose
- Ned_01

Ned_01

Opening a Facebook account when you're 11 is wrong. I mean, he's lying to do that. OK, it's not a mega lie, but it's still a lie. We want this kid to grow up truthful, right? ;)

4.11 PM

- justme
- Firedragon
- Rose

3 **Make notes on the arguments which are given for and against underage use of social media sites.**

✔	✘
1	1
2	2
3	3

4   **Underline the parts of the posts which express the same ideas as these sentences. Which sentences are more appropriate in an essay?**

a) They have not yet developed an awareness of how their actions affect others.

b) It can be difficult to cope with the pressures of social media.

c) We should encourage children to be honest.

d) This is an issue which concerns us all.

e) There are a lot of other ways to enjoy using the Internet.

f) Learning how to use social media is an important life skill.

5   **Complete the sentences about this issue using your own ideas.**

a) More and more children ....

b) The main reason for this is ....

c) Generally, ...

6   **Answer the exam task using information and language from the previous exercises to help you.**

 ## EXAM TASK

In your English class you have been talking about social media. Now your teacher has asked you to write an essay.

Write your essay using **all** the notes and giving reasons for your point of view.

Should there be age restrictions for social media sites?

Notes

Write about:

1. safety

2. emotional pressures

3. .... (your own idea)

Exam tip!

Your writing style for an essay should be quite formal. Avoid informal language and structures.

Digital generation

1   **Look at the opinions about using technology. Have you or someone you know ever said the same things? Discuss in pairs.**

1 Through social media sites we surround ourselves with people who have the same beliefs and likes. These are the only people we can get along with now.

2 I hate it when I see a mother pushing her child on the swing and talking to someone else on the phone at the same time.

3 I stopped to watch some street theatre on my way home. Suddenly I realised I was the only one watching it. Everyone else was filming it.

4 Conversation is spontaneous. You never know what someone will say next. When you chat to someone online, you can control what you say.

5 Who's in charge? The Internet or you?

2   **Match these views with the opinions in exercise 1. Which of these views is NOT expressed?**

   a) We've forgotten how to enjoy the moment. Virtual reality is much more exciting than everyday life.

   b) Virtual reality is much more exciting.

   c) We are losing the art of conversation.

   d) Social media separates us into cliques.

   e) We ignore those around us because we are too busy texting or phoning.

   f) The way we live our lives is being controlled by our technology.

3   **Work in pairs. Think of opposite points of view to those expressed in exercise 2. Write one or two ideas for each item.**

4   **With your partner, complete these sentences using some of your ideas, and the opinions in exercise 2.**

   a) On the one hand, *they can record moments, relive them and share them with friends.* .

   On the other hand, ...

   b) There is no doubt that ....

   However, ...

   c) ....

   In spite of this, ...

   What's more, ...

5   **Which of the phrases in exercise 4 are used to express contrasting points of view? Which phrase is used to provide an additional point of view?**

6 Look at the phrases below. Mark them C (used to signal a *contrasting* point of view) or A (used to signal an *additional* point).

a) Moreover, … ☐

b) Although, … ☐

c) Above all, … ☐

d) On the contrary, … ☐

e) In fact, … ☐

f) Similarly, … ☐

g) …, though. ☐

7 Read the exam task and look at the essay plan. Make notes for each section using the information in this activity and your own ideas. Include phrases you can use to contrast and add further points.

✏ EXAM TASK

In your English class you have been talking about the digital generation. Now your teacher has asked you to write an essay.

Young people live in a world which is increasingly connected, but many of them fail to really communicate. Do you agree?

Notes

Write about:

1. meeting people

2. new technology

3. .... (your own idea)

Write your essay using **all** the notes and giving reasons for your point of view.

Essay plan

Paragraphs	Content notes	Useful phrases
Introduction (give examples of the digital generation)		
First point of view and opposing point of view		
Second point of view and opposing point of view		
Third point of view and opposing point of view		
Conclusion: stating your final point of view		

8 Write your essay.

Exam tip!

There is more than one way to organise your answer. Try this option too:
- *Introduction*
- *First paragraph: negative points*
- *Second paragraph: positive points*
- *Conclusion*

Criminal activity

1 **Use the words from the box to complete the mind maps.**

be charged with   behind bars   break in   burglary   convict   court
personal identity   reoffend   robbery   sentence   smuggle   steal

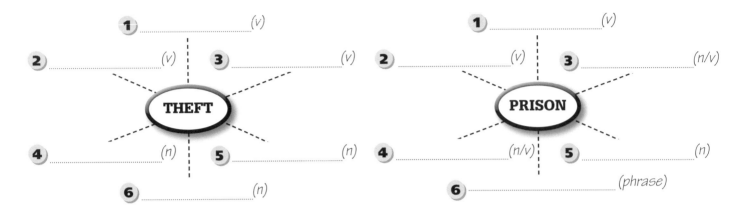

THEFT — 1 .... (v)   2 .... (v)   3 .... (v)   4 .... (n)   5 .... (n)   6 .... (n)

PRISON — 1 .... (v)   2 .... (v)   3 .... (n/v)   4 .... (n/v)   5 .... (n)   6 .... (phrase)

2 **Complete the extracts below with the numbers.**

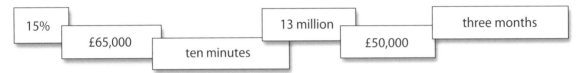

15%   £65,000   ten minutes   13 million   £50,000   three months

profit or to gain some unfair or dishonest advantage.
Identity theft is the fastest-growing crime in the USA. Around **(a)** .... people are affected every year.
Justice, or the administering of deserved punishment or

In recent years, crime rates in the UK have been down by as much as **(b)** ...., meaning burglaries and car crimes are not so common. But these figures don't take into account cyber crime. When online crime was included in the figures for the first time in 2015, crime rates increased by a staggering 107%.

It all started with a letter from a bank saying I was behind in my loan repayments. 'What loan?' I asked. Someone had taken out a loan in my name, using my address and social security number*. This criminal had all my details, and she'd had them for **(c)** .... I was in shock. I think people don't really understand what identity theft is. They think it's when someone steals your credit card and uses it. But this woman had taken out credit, signed up for gas, electricity and phone at her house, all using my details. She'd even got medicine from the doctor.

I was lucky because the criminal was charged. She lived about **(d)** .... from my house. She was given community service, not a prison sentence.
Criminals make a lot of money out of identity theft, but the authorities don't treat it like the serious crime that it is.

*In the USA, a Social Security number is used as a national form of ID.

In the UK it costs around **(e)** .... to imprison a person including police and court costs, plus **(f)** .... for each year they spend behind bars. Less serious crimes are commonly punished by means of fines, community service or drug rehabilitation, which cost considerably less. Around 36% of those on community service end up back in the courts, compared to 60% of those released from short prison sentences.

3 Look at these four sentences. How many different ways can you find to say the same information? Use the words in the box.

> decrease   drop   fall   increase   rise

a There has been a steady fall in burglaries.

b There has been a sudden rise in rates of cyber crime.

c Rates of personal identity theft have gone up dramatically.

d Car crimes are down by 15%.

4 Use the words in the box to rewrite the text below so that it has the same meaning.

> a considerable number of   on a daily basis   the latest   a minority of   most

The majority of people in the UK and USA now use the amazing qualities of the Internet every day, but unfortunately the Internet has also managed to create a new problem: cyber crime. There must be only a very small percentage of households which have not been affected by some kind of cyber crime. Law enforcement agencies worldwide are trying to tackle the problem, but cyber crime is on the increase and many people have become victims of hacking, theft, identity theft and malicious software. All households should make sure they have up-to-date anti-virus and security software on their home systems, but even this is not infallible.

5 Read the exam task and write your essay. Include some general information about crime rates in your answer.

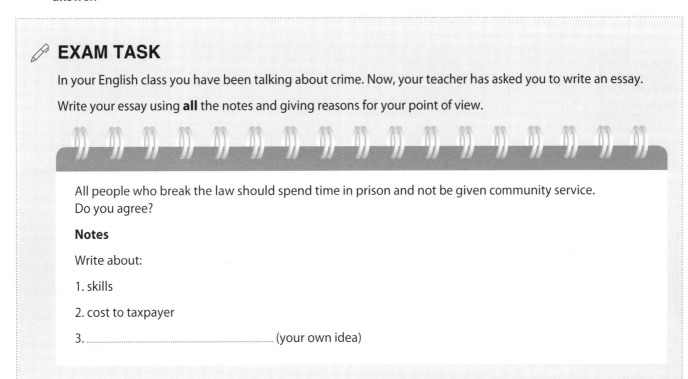

✎ EXAM TASK

In your English class you have been talking about crime. Now, your teacher has asked you to write an essay.

Write your essay using **all** the notes and giving reasons for your point of view.

All people who break the law should spend time in prison and not be given community service. Do you agree?

Notes

Write about:

1. skills

2. cost to taxpayer

3. .... (your own idea)

Celebrity status

1 Look at this website home page and answer the questions.

a) Who is this website aimed at?

b) What style of writing will be used in the articles?

c) Would you be interested in reading something on this site?

2 The following headlines come from a feed on the Y-WOW site. Which are you most likely to click on? Compare your answers with a partner.

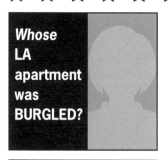

3 Which headlines were you interested in? Why do we follow celebrity gossip? Discuss in pairs.

4   Read this post from the Y-WOW! site and use the article plan to help you think of some ideas for an article.

Here at Y-WOW! we love celebrities and we're so jealous of their lifestyles. But then again, we love a night in with friends too. What about you? Would you swap your lifestyle to be a celeb? Or would you keep your life the way it is? Send us your articles. We'll publish the best one here on the site!

Two points in favour of a celeb lifestyle:

1 ....

2 ....

Further ideas, opinions or examples:

....

....

Two points in favour of keeping life the way it is:

1 ....

2 ....

Further ideas, opinions or examples:

....

....

Conclusion:

....

....

Exam tip!

Spend five to ten minutes at the beginning of the exam task coming up with ideas. It will save you time in the end!

5   Write your article.

6   When you have finished swap articles with a classmate and answer these questions.

Your opinion matters

Did you enjoy reading the article?   ◯ yes   ◯ no

Is this the type of article you would expect to see on this website?   ◯ yes   ◯ no

How would you rate this article?   ◯ awesome   ◯ getting there   ◯ needs work

Taking a gap year

In many English-speaking countries and in Europe it is common to take a year away from your studies, usually between high school and further education or before starting a job. This is called a gap year.

1 **Read what the people say about their gap years. What did they choose to do? What benefits do they mention about taking a gap year?**

I found out about an organisation that runs volunteer programmes helping schoolchildren in Ghana. I was quite apprehensive about whether I could cope at first, but my parents supported me and I talked it through with a couple of my teachers too. The organisation put me in touch with a girl who had taken part in the programme the previous year. It made all the difference. I felt much better prepared and confident. I wouldn't have missed my gap year for the world. I got used to living away from home and it gave me the confidence to try new things and learn from every experience.

My friends were all taking a gap year so it seemed like a good idea. They all got themselves organised, but I didn't really know what I wanted to do. It took me six months to decide and make all the arrangements. I wish I had found out more before my year started – I could have done so much more with it.

I volunteered to help with sea turtle conservation in Mexico. I want to work in conservation so it was an obvious choice for me. I had already applied for my university place before I left. I'm so glad I did because I didn't have to stress about it while I was there. I'm at uni now and I'm so motivated to learn everything about conservation that I can. The best thing about being in Mexico was living with and helping the local people. I learnt so much about the culture that I would never have discovered as a tourist. Whatever you do with your gap year, make sure you enjoy it!

I was really burnt out when I finished college. I didn't really know what jobs to apply for. I'm really glad I took a gap year, not just because I had amazing experiences, but because I became so much more independent and assertive. I went on a four-week language course in Italy and then took a work placement in a hotel. It made a change to find out how the world works rather than just read about it. I'm back home and applying for jobs now and my CV looks so much better with my gap year experiences on it.

2 In pairs, write a list of five tips for someone who is thinking of doing a gap year. Use the information in the texts to help you.

3 Work in pairs. Read the pairs of sentences and discuss which is the most appropriate style for an article with this title: *Gap years: a good use of time or just time off?*

1 **a)** First of all, without the structure that school or college provides, students may not make good use of their time.

   b) So without the structure of school or college, can students still make good use of their time?

2 **a)** You might be surprised to know that your gap year experiences can actually prepare you better for college or work.

   b) Surprisingly, the experiences students gain can prepare them better for college or work.

3 **a)** Taking part in a gap year programme can be expensive.

   b) If students want to take part in a gap year programme, it can be expensive.

4 **a)** The biggest advantage of a gap year can be learning new skills.

   b) For me, the best part of my gap year was learning new skills.

5 **a)** You could improve your high school Spanish by enrolling on a language course in a Spanish-speaking country.

   b) Head for Peru and brush up your Spanish!

4 Read the exam task and write your article.

✐ EXAM TASK

You see this announcement in an English-language magazine:

Articles wanted

Should I take a gap year?

We are looking for articles about gap years. You may have been on a gap year or you may be considering taking one. Tell us about your concerns. Suggestions and tips welcome!

The best articles will be published in next month's magazine.

Write your **article**.

Exam tip!

Have fun writing your article! Make sure your grammar and spelling is correct, but the style for an article can be quite informal.

'Why here? Why now?'

1 Read Eric's blog post and discuss how you would respond in pairs.

Eric_lingo99

Take a look at this fact I found out today: around 600,000 people travel to the UK every year to learn English!!

So that got me thinking. What is the best way to learn a language? Is it doing a language course in the country? Or living abroad for a few years? Watching TV in your target language? Or signing up to a language learning app? Or maybe it's private conversation classes on Skype?

Let me know your views!

2 Look at the exam task below. What does the writer need to include in their answer? Underline the keywords in the exam question.

 EXAM TASK

You see this announcement on the noticeboard of an English language school:

> **Articles wanted**
>
> **WHY HERE? WHY NOW?**
>
> We would love to hear why you have decided to take an English course with us now and why you chose this area.
>
> The best articles will be published on our website.

3 Look at the two sample answers. Which do you prefer?

a

'I have to tell you a serious thing, Mr Ikeda'. Last November a section manager of my ex-company told me this. It made me surprise. The company was bankrupt. That is why I quit my job and came to London.

Then why London? There are two reasons. First of all, I like the English language. In Japan we are usually taught English in the American style. But I like British English because I'm a big fan of British comedy films. This made me decide to come here and study the language through British culture. Secondly, I am interested in British music very much. Every week I listen to the 'official top 40' in Britain.

I have three weeks left before I go back to Japan. I think I have learned and discovered a lot here, which makes me satisfied very much.

b **Why here?**

London is one of the most interesting citys in europe. It is a cultural but also an economic centre. I have been to London four times, but only for business reasons. The more I saw of the city, the more I want to explore it.

Another reason to choose London is, that I know some people here and I look forward to seeing them very much.

I'm interested in history and art. London is a good place to enjoy those to topics because this city lives with his tradition and is full of art.

Why now?

The time now is right because we are starting some international projects and I shall be part of them. My company offered to pay for a language course. The number of our international client's is increasing. While negotiating with them, I felled the need to be more secure in my language skills.

Despite these professional reasons I like to be abroad and I enjoy travelling very much. English is a language, that can help wherever you go.

4 Complete feedback forms for the writers. Be sensitive in your feedback!

Feedback Form	A	B
STYLE		
Is it the right style for an article? Why / Why not.		
ANSWERING THE QUESTION		
Does the article answer the key points in the question?		
Are all the points relevant?		
Is it about the right length?		
LANGUAGE		
Give examples of good vocabulary the writer has used.		
Has the writer used a variety of structures?		
Give examples of any spelling or grammar you would correct.		

5 Compare your feedback with a partner and ask your teacher to show you some sample feedback from the answers.

6 Write your own answer for the exam task. When you have finished, swap answers with another student and give them your feedback.

Exam tip!

When you finish the exam task, take five minutes to review and check your work. Use the criteria on the feedback form to help you!

Take sleep seriously!

1 Research projects, assignments, presentations ... how do you cope? When there's work to be done, it's easy to cut back on sleep and do without breaks. Have you ever said any of these things? Compare your answers in pairs.

I chatted with friends on Facebook.

I research information on my iPad in bed before I go to sleep.

I stayed up so late working on this project!

When I get to the end of a piece of work, I have a treat or go out for a walk.

So long as I get a good night's sleep I can handle anything.

I've worked so hard on this. I was on the computer for six hours yesterday!

2 Look at this article about sleep. Is the article easy to read? Why? / Why not?

Sleep Training

Research suggests that many teenagers are getting just five hours of sleep a night. Teachers report teenagers falling asleep in class and many keep their energy levels up with sugary drinks and snacks. But it's not just teenagers. The recommended number of hours of sleep for adults is seven to nine, yet a survey conducted by the National Sleep Foundation in the US found 39% of people in the UK and 66% of Japanese people slept for less than seven hours on work nights. The cortex – the part of the brain which controls thinking, speech and memory – needs time off at the end of the day. Without sleep, we become forgetful, less able to maintain conversations and find it harder to concentrate. Long-term sleep loss makes us more vulnerable to illness and mood swings. A study of the sleeping habits of 12 to 18 year olds shows that those that sleep less than five hours a night are 70% more likely to suffer depression. So why do we do it? In today's society we are constantly pushing ourselves to achieve more, and cutting into our sleeping time is inevitable. Many of us are using our smartphones way into the night to keep in touch, keep up-to-date and not miss out. Stimulants like caffeine and sugar are delaying our sleep at night. Believe it or not, there's now a thing called sleep-training. And their advice is: get some exercise during the day and don't nap in the afternoon. Eat a full meal in the early evening and avoid eating chocolate or drinking coffee before bed. Don't text, use a computer or watch TV for half an hour before going to bed and sleep somewhere which is not too warm and not too bright. In short, it's time we started to look after ourselves and take sleep seriously.

3   **Look at the writer's plan for their article. Divide the article into paragraphs according to the plan.**

> Introduction: Lack of sleep in today's world, examples of teenagers and adults
>
> Paragraph 1: Why do we need sleep?
>
> Paragraph 2: Why are we not sleeping enough?
>
> Paragraph 3: What advice is there for getting more sleep?
>
> Conclusion: Short and snappy: take sleep seriously.

4   **Read the exam task and write a plan using the outline below. What questions are you going to answer in each paragraph?**

 EXAM TASK

You see this announcement on the noticeboard of an English language school:

> **Articles wanted**
>
> **SLEEP AND ME**
>
> We want to hear your views. Do you get enough sleep? If not, why not? And what are you going to do about it? Or are you happy with your sleep routine? Tell us why you think sleep is important and share your tips for a good night's sleep.
>
> The best articles will be published online.

Introduction: ....

Paragraph 1: ....

Paragraph 2: ....

Paragraph 3: ....

Conclusion: ....

5   **Discuss your plan in pairs. Are your plans similar?**

6   **Write your article.**

Exam tip!

A text with no paragraphs can be confusing and difficult to read. Make one or two points in each main paragraph.

Hallowe'en: A time to have fun

1 Read the exam task and Rita's sample answer. Then answer the questions.

 EXAM TASK

You see this announcement on an English-language website:

Articles wanted

CELEBRATE!

We are looking for articles about festivities in different countries. Describe a celebration in your country and explain what people do. Say why you like it or don't like it.

The best article will win a prize!

Every year millions of Americans celebrate Hallowe'en and the fun is going around the world. I'm going to tell you why it's so good.

I've lived in America for two years now and Hallowe'en here is very nice. It's a very big holiday. It's not only a children's party now. Teenagers and adults love it too. Everyone takes part.

Hallowe'en is not a religious festival. The name comes from All Hallows Eve. The traditional symbol of Hallowe'en is the Jack O'Lantern. Every year I have a pumpkin. I make eyes in it and a bad smile. I put a candle inside the pumpkin. I put it in the front yard. Local children dress up. They come for sweets and ask 'Trick or treat!'.

Hallowe'en is good because it is fun. It's good to dress up. You can come to America for Hallowe'en. Then you can have fun and not worry about the neighbours!

a) Did you enjoy reading the article? Why? / Why not?

b) Do you think this article will win a prize? Why? / Why not?

2a Rita wants to win the article competition. Look at these ways she can improve the text.

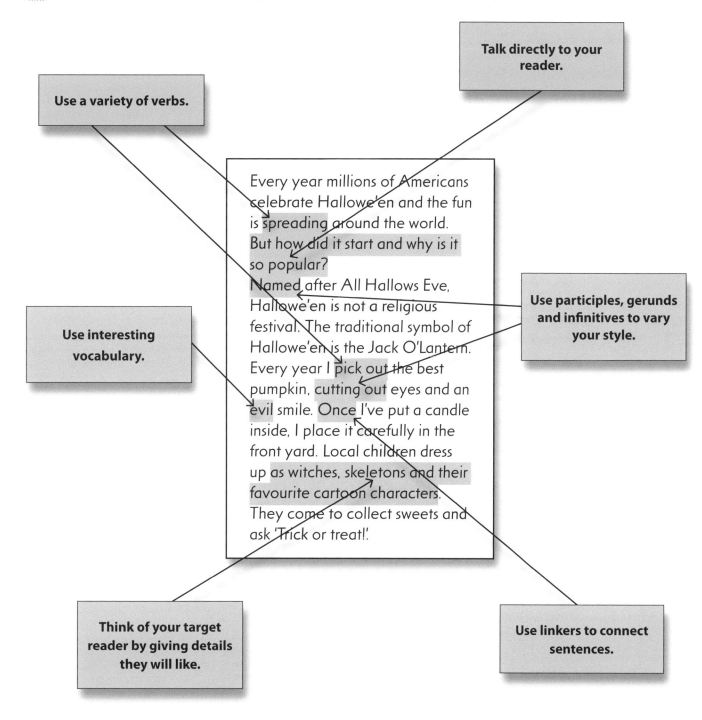

Talk directly to your reader.

Use a variety of verbs.

Use interesting vocabulary.

Use participles, gerunds and infinitives to vary your style.

Think of your target reader by giving details they will like.

Use linkers to connect sentences.

Every year millions of Americans celebrate Hallowe'en and the fun is spreading around the world. But how did it start and why is it so popular?
Named after All Hallows Eve, Hallowe'en is not a religious festival. The traditional symbol of Hallowe'en is the Jack O'Lantern. Every year I pick out the best pumpkin, cutting out eyes and an evil smile. Once I've put a candle inside, I place it carefully in the front yard. Local children dress up as witches, skeletons and their favourite cartoon characters. They come to collect sweets and ask 'Trick or treat!'.

2b Now read the last two paragraphs of Rita's answer in exercise 1 again. Can you help Rita improve on them?

3 Now it's your turn. Write the article about a celebration in your country.

Useful language

Ask anyone what they like best about …
… is the part I like the best.
my favourite time of year
It wouldn't be … without …
It's a time to …
What could be better than … ?

Exam tip!

Show off your vocabulary and a variety of structures in the article task!

Never give up!

Parkour (or freerunning) is the act of moving freely over and through any area using only the abilities of the body. Parkour is both a physical practice and a philosophy. People who practise parkour are known as 'traceurs' and many of them feel it has changed their lives.

1 Read Zack's post and underline the phrases and verbs he uses to compare his life now with his life before he discovered parkour.

Topic: How parkour changed my life

» *June 11, 02.34 PM*

'There's nothing like parkour. It's had a big effect on me. I've stopped smoking, my diet has improved and I know more about exercise now too. I'm a friendlier person, definitely happier and more relaxed … I've met so many new friends, people who have welcomed me with open arms. Even my relationship with my family is much better.

As a traceur, I try to follow the philosophy as much as possible. When I train harder, my everyday outlook changes. Any obstacle can be overcome. Never give up. Pace yourself and gradually you will be able to push your limits even further.'

Zack, 27

---

2 Check your underlined phrases in pairs. Ask your teacher for the answers. Then replace each comparative phrase with a phrase that has a similar meaning from the box below.

> more amiable   as much as I can   far better   certainly more cheerful   changed me a lot   more easy-going
>
> have a greater understanding of   has got healthier   more intensely   more and more

3 Write your article. Include some comparative phrases in your answer.

✏ EXAM TASK

You see this announcement in an English-language magazine for young people:

Articles wanted

ME TIME!

We'd like you to tell us about a free-time activity you take part in.

We'd like to know how you got started and what benefits it has had for you.

The best articles will be published in next month's magazine.

Exam tip!

Any of the exam tasks in the First Writing exam could ask you to make comparisons.

4 Swap your article with a partner. How many comparative phrases did he/she use? Are they used appropriately? Which is the best one?

Learning something new

1 Discuss in pairs. Have you been on a training or holiday course recently? Did you enjoy the course? Why / Why not? What courses would you like to do?

2 In your opinion which of these are most important in a successful course?

- learning a skill you need
- hands-on training
- lots of hand-outs to take home
- sharing experiences with others
- regular tests
- a good trainer

3 Liam went on a course to learn new IT skills for his work in a tourist office. Complete his feedback form.

Comments

a) The trainer knew a lot about his subject, but didn't know how to get this across.

Therefore, ...

b) The pace of the session was very slow. As a result, ...

c) Due to the fact that the Internet wasn't working, ...

d) Since the course finished an hour early, ...

e) I left the course without having learnt very much. For this reason, ...

4 Compare your answers in pairs. Have you ever had a similar experience of training?

5 Look at this exam task. The conclusion has already been written. Write your report and use the conclusion given. Try to use some of the linkers from exercise 3 in your answer.

✎ EXAM TASK

You recently went on a first-aid course. The aim of the course was to give you basic first aid and advice on what to do when faced with an emergency.

You have been asked to write a report for your manager. Your report should:

- include whether the event achieved its aim
- recommend whether the company should book other colleagues onto this course

Conclusion:

First-aid training is an essential skill at work and we were all motivated to learn, but unfortunately none of my colleagues felt we learned very much on the course. For this reason, I would recommend arranging another first-aid course, but not with this particular company.

Exam tip!

It is usual to include some disadvantages or negative feedback in your report – but don't overdo it! Aim for a balanced view.

A vibrant city

1   You are considering going on a study course in the UK for three months. When deciding where to go, which three things on this list are most important to you?

- historical town
- near countryside
- good nightlife
- close to an airport

- a choice of language schools
- well-connected by rail
- plenty of places to eat
- successful football team

- wide range of shops
- somewhere well-known
- excellent hospital
- other: _____

2   Compare your ideas with a partner. Did your partner choose the same things? Why? / Why not?

3   Read the article. Which items on the list in exercise 1 are mentioned?

OUR CITY REPORTER

Name: Tom Bailey

Lives: I live in Leeds, a city in Yorkshire, in the north of England.

Favourite waste of time: Chilling with my mates in the park.

Typical phrase: 'Yo!' It's how I greet most people.

Q: What is Leeds famous for?
Tom: Nowadays Leeds is probably best-known as a great shopping destination! It's been voted the best place to shop in the whole of the UK, beating London! Other than that, Leeds is a brilliant place for a night out, because of the many nightclubs and venues in the city.

Q: What do you love and hate about your city?
Tom: I love Leeds because it's a big, vibrant city and the locals are really friendly and helpful.

The only thing that bugs me is the traffic – it clogs up the city centre at rush hour and if you're stuck in your car, it just feels like you're wasting time.

Of course, like any big city there are areas I wouldn't really feel safe walking around, such as Chapel Town or Harehills, but these are not areas you would go to by accident if you were visiting the city.

LOCATION Leeds is near three national parks (areas of protected countryside) and is only one hour from Manchester and two hours from London by train. It also has its own international airport.

SHOPPING: The Trinity Centre You'll need money to burn here! There are 120 shops, cinemas and cafes.

BUILDINGS Many of the important buildings in the city centre are from Victorian times, such as the Leeds market building.

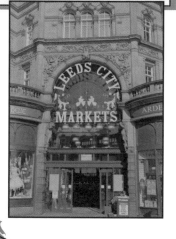

Leeds

DID YOU KNOW? With around 750,000 inhabitants, Leeds is the third largest city in the UK.

LEARNING ENGLISH There are a number of English language schools in Leeds. The schools, which are often small and independent, offer a good range of English language courses and a personal approach to learning.

---

4   Rebecca's boss has asked her to write a report about Leeds, including information on the amenities in Leeds and whether the city would be a good place for students to learn English. Complete Rebecca's report, using information from Tom's article.

To: Managing Director, City Schools

From: Rebecca Lacey

Subject: Leeds, Yorkshire

Introduction
The aim of this report is to outline the suitability of Leeds as a destination for language students.

Location and transport links
Leeds is well-connected and is only two hours from London by train. a) .... However, most direct flights are to Europe only. It is close to three national parks which are easily reached.

Town centre amenities
The centre of Leeds is of historical interest but it also has some excellent modern amenities, including the modern Trinity Centre which has 120 stores, and a wide variety of nightclubs and venues. Many people come from outside Leeds to shop, and for this reason b) ....

Language schools and student life
None of the language schools in Leeds are very well-known. On the other hand, c) ....

Despite the fact that d) ...., the locals are friendly and helpful and students should receive a warm welcome in host families. The city is generally safe, although e) ....

Conclusion
Leeds has a lot of points in its favour and would be a very good base for students wishing to learn English and explore the UK further.

5   Underline the phrases in exercise 3 which are used to link your new information to the rest of the text.

6   Read the exam task and write your report.

✎ EXAM TASK

A well-known language school is considering opening a new school in a town or city in your country. Students would come from all over the world to study your language. The language school has asked you to write a report about the suitability of one city for the school.

Your report should:

- include information about what students can do in the town / city
- recommend whether the town / city would be a good place for a language student

Useful language

Opening phrases

As requested, ...
The aim / purpose of this report is to ... (and to ...) .
This report looks at ...

An eco-friendly home

1 **Look at the diagram showing features of an eco-friendly home. Which of these features have you seen in your area?**

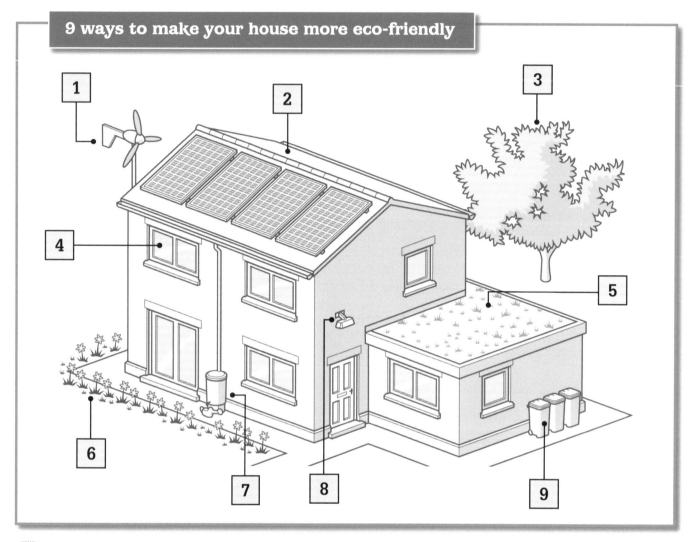

9 ways to make your house more eco-friendly

2 **Match these descriptions with the features on the house.**

a) Collect water from water butts for use in gardens. ⑦

b) Native plants will attract native insects like bees and butterflies. The spread of non-native insect species has had a severe effect around the world. ☐

c) Electricity produced by the wind via a micro wind turbine can be stored in a battery. ☐

d) Keep heat in with double glazing and save a lot of wasted energy. ☐

e) Plant a tree in your garden and you've got a place where birds can rest. Ask your neighbour to plant one too and you've got a habitat. ☐

f) Solar energy from panels can provide enough electricity for your own needs. ☐

g) Include a separate bin for food waste. Food waste that goes to landfill produces methane (a greenhouse gas). ☐

h) A green roof will improve air quality for yourself and your neighbours. ☐

i) Turning off your outside lights reduces electricity bills and is less disorientating for migrating birds. ☐

3 Look at the disadvantages below. Which features in the diagram do they refer to?

a) The installation of these can be expensive and it could take ten years before your investment starts to save you money.

b) Animals like foxes and rats can be attracted to them.

c) Turning off yours may not make a large difference. It needs to be a city-wide policy.

d) An annual inspection is needed to remove unwanted plants and check there are no roots which could cause leaks.

e) In many urban locations, they do not generate significant amounts of power.

4 Based on what you have read, make recommendations for using two of the above features in your local area.

In general, ...

I would definitely recommend that ....

....

....

Generally, ...

I would therefore recommend that ....

....

5 Read the exam task and write your report in 140–190 words.

✏ EXAM TASK

Your local council is considering making buildings and gardens in your local area more environmentally-friendly. You have been asked to write a report. Your report should:

- include different ways buildings and gardens in the area can become more eco-friendly
- recommend which ways could easily be implemented in your area

Write your **report**.

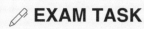
Exam tip!

A final recommendation in a report will often include a generalisation introduced by a phrase, such as Generally ...,, In general ... or On the whole ... .

The next best thing

1   **Look at the inventions. Complete each text using the verbs in the box. Be careful! Some of the verbs need to be in the passive form.**

A   The dance-powered phone charger

If your phone **(1)** *runs out* of battery at a music festival, this could be a solution. The band **(2)** .... someone's arm. As the person dances, the storage battery **(3)** .... Then the mobile phone **(4)** .... to the storage battery.

> charge up   connect   put on   ~~run out~~

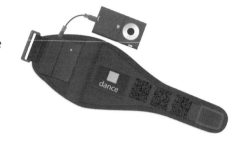

B   The instant bird feeder

A loaf of bread **(1)** .... on the chopping board. As the bread **(2)** ...., the crumbs **(3)** .... a long tube. The tube leads outside, where the crumbs **(4)** .... by the local birds.

> cut   eat   go down   place

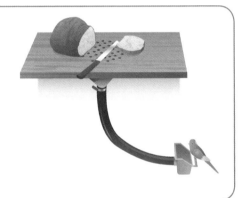

C   Recycling made easy

About forty sheets of paper **(1)** .... into the machine. The paper **(2)** .... and then **(3)** .... in water. About thirty minutes later, a roll of freshly-made toilet paper **(4)** ....

> dissolve   insert   produce   shred

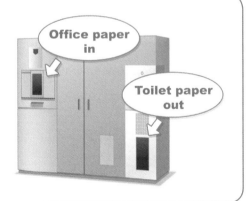

Office paper in

Toilet paper out

D   The pool computer

The pool computer **(1)** .... in a swimming pool. The computer **(2)** .... by solar energy so it does not need **(3)** .... The computer has a touchscreen so it does not **(4)** .... a keyboard.

> float   plug in   power   require

---

2   Work in groups of four: one boss and three salespeople.

The salespeople

Choose one of the inventions each. Describe how the product works to your group and explain why the company should sell it. Think about the appeal and selling-points of the product for consumers.

The boss

You work for a company that sells interesting inventions. You are looking for the next best thing! Which invention do you like best?

3   Read the exam task and write your report. Include some passive voice forms in your answer. Challenge: can you write the report without using the word 'you'?

 EXAM TASK

> You work for a company that sells interesting inventions. Your boss has asked for a report on three ideas which inventors have submitted to the company. Your report should:
>
> - include information on how each invention works
> - make recommendations for the best product for your company to sell
>
> Write your **report**.

4   Swap reports with a partner. Read your partner's report and answer the questions.

Seriously …

a) Does the report give a balanced view of the products (some good points and some negative points)?

b) Are there any examples of the passive voice (correctly used)?

c) Is the conclusion clear and logical?

For fun …

d) Did the report contain the word 'you'?

e) Which phrase from the report do you wish you had written in *your* report?

f) Would you buy the product the report recommends?

Exam tip!

The passive voice is often a feature of more formal writing, e.g. reports.

A must-see film

1 **How many films can you think of that were based on a book? Did you prefer the book or the film? Discuss in pairs.**

2 **Read the short reviews of a book and a film. Do you know the titles?**

This film, directed by Danny Boyle, won eight Oscars and is both beautiful and shocking. Set in India, it is about the experiences of eighteen-year-old Jamal. Jamal, played by Dev Patel, is a believable character whose experiences will tug on your heartstrings. The film also examines the complicated relationship between Dev and his older brother, Salim. The film is fast-paced and colourful with a dazzling soundtrack. I definitely recommend it.

This best-selling novel by Vikas Swarup was the inspiration behind an Oscar-winning film. The story is about an orphan who appears on a quiz show in India and, to everyone's surprise, answers twelve questions correctly to win a big money prize. The author uses the twelve questions as an original way of telling the story of the orphan's life. The story is reasonably fast-moving, and the characters are memorable. It gives the reader insights into both the good and bad sides of Indian society.

3 **Choose the correct definition for words in the reviews.**

  a) orphan: a child with no parents / an only child

  b) be inspiration for the film: gave the director the idea for the film / was written after the film was released

  c) original: traditional / new and different

  d) memorable: worth remembering / hard to remember

  e) insight into: criticism of / understanding of

  f) tug on your heartstrings: make you have sympathy for / make you feel shocked

  g) complex: unhappy / complicated

  h) dazzling: unusual / stunning

  i) believable: a character who always believes what others say / you can believe this character exists

4   Underline the adjectives in each review. Does the review writer prefer the book or the film?

5   Look at the phrases. Which can be used to talk about a film, a book or both? Write F for film, B for book and FB for film / book.

☐ It's about …

☐ It takes place in …

☐ It is set in …

☐ It tells the story of …

☐ It's (expertly) directed by …

☐ It is based on …

☐ It's (beautifully) written by …

☐ It stars … as …

☐ There are exceptional / mediocre performances from …

☐ It's full of wonderful / stereotypical / comic characters.

☐ The images will stay long in the reader's mind.

☐ It has an unexpected / a predictable ending when …

☐ It had the audience laughing out loud.

☐ I couldn't put it down.

☐ It's a must-see.

☐ It's well worth reading.

☐ If you only read one book this year, make sure it's …

6   Work in your pairs. Choose one of the books and films you discussed in exercise 1. Talk about the book or film using the phrases in the list.

7   Write your review using some of the phrases and adjectives from exercises 3 and 4. Write between 140 and 190 words.

✎ EXAM TASK

You recently saw this notice on an international film website for teenagers:

> **Reviews wanted**
>
> We're looking for reviews of films that are based on a book. Tell us a little about the book and the film, how they differ, which you preferred and why.
>
> The best reviews will appear on our website next month.

Exam tip!

Stick to the recommended word count. If you write too much, the examiner may not read the last part of your answer. If you write too little and don't answer everything in the task, you will lose marks.

First-rate food

1 What type of food do you enjoy when you eat out? Do you choose food from your own country or from another culture?

2a You ask your friend what she thinks of a particular restaurant. She says, 'It's OK.' Is this a positive comment or not? Discuss in pairs.

2b Now group the adjectives and phrases from the word box.

Fantastic! ☆☆☆☆	Good ☆☆☆	OK ☆☆	Horrible ☆

acceptable amazing awful disgusting dreadful dull excellent exceptional first-rate
forgettable horrid memorable not bad nothing special out of this world reasonable
satisfactory shocking so-so stunning tasty terrible

3 Complete the sentences.

a) All of the adjectives and phrases can be used in this sentence: The meal was ....

b) Which can't be used in this sentence? It was a/an .... meal.

4 Read the exam task. Underline the key words in the question.

✏ EXAM TASK

You recently saw this announcement on an English-language website:

Write a review about a café or restaurant which serves food from a particular country or culture. Describe the quality of the food and the atmosphere. Say how it is typical of food from the country and whether you recommend it.

The best reviews will be included on our website.

5   Choose a café or restaurant to write about. It can be one you know, or you can invent one. Look at the checklist and choose three things to include in your review.

☐ how to find the place   ☐ the music that was played

☐ one or two dishes from the menu   ☐ when it is open

☐ what the service is like   ☐ whether the menu is expensive

☐ how the place is decorated   ☐ whether the place is popular

☐ who you went with   ☐ what type of event the place is good for

                                       ☐ what type of meal the place is good for

Exam tip!

There is a lot of information that can be included in a restaurant review. Check that you write the information that the question asks for.

6   Write your review using the information from the checklist. Try to include one or two adjectives from exercise 2.

7   Swap your reviews with a partner. Read your partner's review and complete the review card with marks out of five (1= terrible, 5 = fantastic).

For food quality, this establishment scores ☐ out of five.

The reviewer gives this establishment ☐ out of five for atmosphere.

Overall this restaurant is

disappointing   ◯

nothing special   ◯

worth a visit   ◯

highly recommended   ◯

Gamer or n00b?

1a Look at the gaming expressions and words. Tick the ones you know the meaning of. Compare with a partner and describe the meanings of the words you know.

ARE YOU A GAMER?

HOW MANY OF THESE TERMS DO YOU KNOW?

- bug ☐
- MMO ☐
- Easter eggs ☐
- expansion ☐
- f2p ☐
- fan-base ☐
- First-Person Shooter ☐
- gameplay ☐
- graphics ☐
- level cap ☐
- n00b ☐
- RPG ☐

1b Ask your teacher for the answers and check your score.

SCORES:

10–12: You know your stuff! (Is there more to life than gaming?)

5–9: More than just a passing interest …

1–4: So if you decide gaming's for you, at least you know where to start.

0: Umm … no. Not your bag.

2 Read the review and answer True or False.

a) *World of Warcraft* is produced by BioWare. **True / False**

b) There was nothing good about *Star Wars: The Old Republic*. **True / False**

c) A lot of people like the Star Wars stories and characters. **True / False**

d) The new MMO was instantly popular. **True / False**

e) There were too many levels in *Star Wars: The Old Republic*. **True / False**

f) Bioware quickly brought out an additional game **True / False**

g) *Star Wars: The Old Republic* is a successful game. **True / False**

When BioWare released MMO (Massively Multiplayer Online) *Star Wars: The Old Republic (SWORT)*, many people thought the reign of Blizzard's *World of Warcraft (WoW)* as the best MMO was over. It wasn't.

The new game had a lot of points in its favour. There were solid graphics and voice acting. The fan-base was huge, the budget even greater, and it was a big hit on its release with an incredible one million players within its first three days.

So what went wrong? The major issue was that BioWare hadn't predicted how quickly players would reach the level cap and they didn't have any plans for dealing with that. As a result, subscribers to the game never reached more than 1.7 million (compare this with *WoW*'s ten million). It wasn't until eighteen months later that the first expansion, *Rise of the Hutt Cartel*, was released. By this time, most players had moved onto other games and didn't look back.

BioWare's game designers should have known better. Although *SWTOR* is not unsuccessful, it has not really lived up to its promise.

3 Look at the exam task. Think of a computer game and make notes about its good points and weak points.

✎ EXAM TASK

You recently saw this notice on an English-language gaming website:

Reviews wanted

Could you do better?

Have you played a new computer game and found it disappointing? Write a review for others telling us what is good about it as well as what could be improved and how.

We have ten PC game subscriptions to give to the best reviews!

4 Write your review. Choose sentences from the list below to start off one or two of your paragraphs.

- [ ] It had plenty of promise.
- [ ] It seemed like such a good idea.
- [ ] So what went wrong?
- [ ] Sadly, I found the game disappointing.
- [ ] .ᵗ had a lot of points in its favour.
- [ ] Let's look at the positives.
- [ ] Has the game lived up to the hype?
- [ ] So should you play it?

5 Find a classmate who knows this game. Does your partner agree with your review?

'Don't miss it!'

1   **Read the review about an art exhibition. What star rating do you think the reviewer gave the exhibition?**

'Henri Matisse: The Cut-Outs' was the most popular exhibition ever held at the Tate Modern, with over half a million visitors. The exhibition featured some of Matisse's best-known art, created in the final years of his life, using shapes cut from sheets of paper.

The light, bright rooms of the iconic Tate Modern were a perfect setting for the works. The huge colourful pictures using naturally inspired shapes, are simple but beautiful. They are a celebration of life, just as the artist intended. Many visitors left the exhibition with huge smiles.

The exhibition was disappointing in only one respect: it was very difficult to actually see the pictures through the heads of the other visitors. The gallery introduced timed tickets to keep the audience moving, but this was not enough to reduce the overcrowding. By the end of the exhibition, real patience was required to endure the queue to buy posters and cards at the shop.

In spite of the crowds, 'Henri Matisse: The Cut-Outs' was an exhibition not to be missed. But the only way to really appreciate it was to follow the example of many visitors and go back more than once.

Tell us your views.

In the past decade, many galleries have organised 'blockbuster' exhibitions of well-loved artists to attract visitors, but there have been many problems with overcrowding. Some say galleries could try showing one- or two-picture exhibitions in one room of their permanent exhibition space and could look at lowering the entry fee. Galleries might want to operate a queuing system so that visitors in the room are limited.

Have your say about exhibitions of the future. Sign in to comment.

2   **Which of these features of a successful exhibition are mentioned in the review?**

visitor numbers ☐   location of site ☐

site or building ☐   ticket policy ☐

ticket pricing ☐   advertising ☐

interactive content ☐   enjoyment (or not) ☐

catering facilities ☐   merchandise, e.g. t-shirts, postcards ☐

3   **What points does the reviewer make about the exhibition?**

⊕ the plus points	⊖ the disappointments	Suggestions / recommendations

4   In the 'Tell us your views' section, which phrases does the reviewer use to make recommendations for changes?

5   Read the exam task and think of an exhibition you have been to which would be appropriate for this review.

 EXAM TASK

You recently saw this notice on an English-language website:

> **Reviews wanted**
>
> **Don't miss it!**
>
> We're looking for reviews of exhibitions or attractions. It could be in a museum, an art gallery or a visitor attraction.
>
> Tell us what you went to, what was good about it, and what features could be improved too.
>
> The best reviews will be put on our website.

6   Make notes about the exhibition. Make recommendations for change using phrases from the Useful Language box.

⊕ the plus points	⊖ the disappointments	Suggestions / recommendations

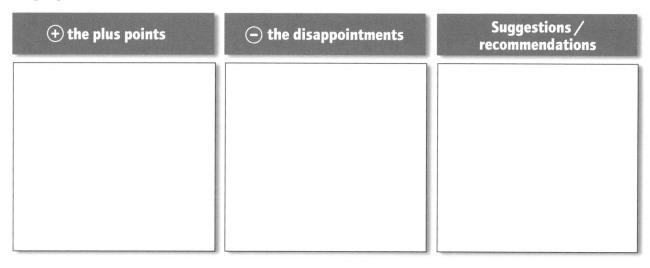

Useful language

They could look at / think about …
They could try …
What I would do is …
They might want / need (to) …

Exam tip!

If you don't know enough facts for your exam task review, then you can make some up – it doesn't all have to be true!

7   Write your review.

8   Swap reviews with a partner and answer the questions.

   a)   Would you like to go to this exhibition? Why?

   b)   What changes does the reviewer recommend?

   c)   What phrases are used to make recommendations for change?

Songs on a playlist

1 Write down the top three songs on your playlist right now and two you definitely wouldn't have on it.

2 Jules is talking about some music tracks. Grade each of her sentences using the key below.

> **1** = strongly dislike   **4** = neutral
>
> **2** = dislike   **5** = like
>
> **3** = dislike a little   **6** = strongly like

a) I'm really into it. ☐

b) I don't think much of it. ☐

c) I can't stand it. ☐

d) I'm not keen on it. ☐

e) It's not my thing. ☐

f) I really don't like it. ☐

g) I don't really like it. ☐

h) I'm mad / crazy about it. ☐

i) I don't mind it. ☐

j) It grows on you. ☐

k) It's never off my playlist. ☐

l) It's my kind of music. ☐

m) I can take it or leave it. ☐

n) It's too … for my liking. ☐

3 Work in pairs. Discuss the songs on your lists using phrases from exercise 2 and items from the Useful Language box.

> **Useful language**
>
> They could look at / think about …
> They could try …
> What I would do is …
> They might want / need (to) …
> It cheers me up.
> It gets you dancing.
>
> It reminds me of …
> It makes me think of …
> I've gone off it.
> I haven't heard it.
> I don't know it.

4 Look at the exam task. Write about a gig you have been to or imagine what it was like to be there – perhaps you have seen a video of it.

✎ EXAM TASK

You recently saw this notice on an English-language website for young people.

> **Playing live**
>
> We want to know who you think is the best singer or band playing live right now. Write a review of a gig by the musician(s). Describe what it was like and don't forget to tell us about your favourite song(s) from the event.
>
> The best reviews will be posted on our site.

Write your **review**.

'I'm so fed up!'

1 **Which English word can be used in all of these sentences? What is the difference in meaning?**

a) I'm .... I didn't mean to step on your toe.

b) Did you hear the news about Jack? I'm really .... for him.

c) I'm .... that you are leaving.

d) ....? What did you say?

e) .... to bother you, but have you got the time?

2 **Match the phrases to the language functions. Which of the phrases are more formal?**

1 Thanks, that would be great.

2 Sorry for the delay in replying.

3 I'd love to.

4 Unfortunately, I am unable to attend. Please accept my apologies.

5 I'm really sorry to hear about what happened.

6 Thank you for your email of 7th September.

7 I'm afraid I'm away that day.

8 I would be delighted to attend.

a) apologising

b) expressing sympathy

c) giving thanks

d) accepting an invitation

e) rejecting an invitation

3 **Look at these extracts from emails. Which of the phrases in exercise 2 could you use in reply?**

a) We've had some bad news. Sophie is currently in hospital.

b) I would be very pleased if you could come to a buffet dinner in aid of charity.

c) I'm writing to ask if you could come to a meeting here on 20 March.

d) Would you like to come round next Friday?

4 **Read the exam task. Underline the parts of the email that need replying to.**

> **Exam tip!**
>
> *Look out for any news in the exam task that needs a response. Use appropriate language to reply.*

 EXAM TASK

You have received this email from your English-speaking friend, Sophie.

From: Sophie

Subject: Fed up!

As you know, I usually go running every day, but I had an accident last week. I had a bad fall and I can't walk very well. I'm getting about OK, but the doctor has said that I can't do any sport for three months. I'm so fed up!

I'll be in your area next week. Have you got any suggestions of things I could do? Why don't you come too?

Write your **email.**

Volunteering

1 **Read the information about volunteering. In pairs talk about any information which surprises / does not surprise you.**

> 'Volunteering is at the very core of being a human. No one has made it through life without someone else's help.'
>
> Heather French Henry, Miss America 2000

vol•un•teer *(v)* to offer help without expecting payment

> Helping is its own reward. It's surprising how it just feels right.'
>
> Paul Newman, U.S. actor

Volunteer

The United States has a long history of volunteering. Nearly a quarter of the population, that's around 62 million people, are volunteers. Around 18.5% of people between 20 and 24 volunteer each year.

Volunteering can include driving a neighbour to hospital, serving meals to the homeless or teaching disadvantaged children. Some of the most popular volunteer activities are fundraising, food distribution, collecting or distributing clothing or working in sports or art groups.

The volunteer rate in the USA is declining, from around 29% of the population in 2003 to around 25% in 2013.

vol•un•teer *(n)* someone who is prepared to do a job without being paid

2 **Imagine you are in charge of recruiting new volunteers for a cancer charity. A potential volunteer has phoned you to ask if you have any vacancies. In pairs write the questions to her replies below.**

a) My uncle was recently diagnosed with cancer. I would like the chance to help others in the same situation. I'm also looking forward to working as part of a team.

b) You raise money to help support people whose relatives are ill with cancer.

c) I can only help out for one afternoon a week.

d) I love playing on my X-box or keeping in touch with friends!

e) I'm really good at playing the guitar.

f) I can walk, but if the work is far from here, I'd need a lift.

3 **Now imagine the volunteer has some questions for you. How will you answer them?**

a) What do you expect of me?

b) What can I expect to get from doing this work?

c) How many hours do you expect me to volunteer each week?

4   **Read the exam task below. What is Noah asking for?**

     a) advice   **b)** information   **c)** news

 EXAM TASK

This is part of an email you have received from your American friend, Noah.

> I've been getting bored at the weekend and my mum suggested I do some volunteer work. I don't know who to volunteer for. Do you have any ideas? And how do you think I should apply?
>
> Thanks,
>
> Noah

5   **Lee has had the following ideas for the exam task. In pairs, use the phrases in the Useful Language box to give advice to Noah.**

- make a list of your interests and skills
- look up some charities you are interested in
- find out if any of these charities have a local group
- do a search on localvolunteer.com
- check out the college noticeboard because there are always adverts on there

6   **Write your email.**

Exam tip!

Look out for questions in the tasks such as: Have you got any ideas? Can you give me any advice? What should I do? *These tasks are asking for advice.*

Useful language

Giving advice
I think you should …
It might help to …
It would be a good idea to …
Have you thought of … (verb + -ing)?
If I were you, I'd …
I think it would be better to …
Hope that helps!

'Where should I stay?'

1 Read these reviews from a travel guide about Edinburgh. Think of a colleague or fellow student. Which place would be best for them to stay in? What about an elderly relative?

94 DR is a bit far from the town centre but don't let that put you off. You are guaranteed a warm welcome from the owners, who are very proud of their breakfast menu – all freshly cooked to order. While some guests may find the spacious rooms a little on the expensive side, others return time after time. Check out availability well in advance as rooms get booked up quickly.

Cityroomz is an excellent hotel on Princes Street. The airline bus stop is right next to the hotel and Haymarket railway station is just a ten-minute walk up the road. The rooms are modern, comfortable and great value. The decoration is a little unusual but there is everything you need for a good night's sleep. All in all, this is a great and budget-friendly place to stay.

SYHA Edinburgh Central is not your average youth hostel. It manages to combine the comfort of a hotel with the relaxed feel of a hostel. The hostel itself is in a great location. The rooms are clean, comfortable and excellent value, although party-goers might find the area is a bit quiet at night. Breakfast is good value but is not included in the price.

2 Now think about your hometown. Which places would you suggest visiting and which hotels would you recommend staying in for the people in the chart? Complete the chart in your notebook. An example answer is given.

Who?	Place to stay	Why?	Be aware that …	Place to go	Why?	Be aware that …
A 19-year-old cousin	Westend Hostel Vienna	good value, plenty of young people stay there	area might be a bit quiet at night	Mariahilferstrasse, Vienna's most popular shopping street	I know she likes shopping	most shops are not open on a Sunday
A good friend						
An elderly relative						
A business colleague						

3 Work in pairs. Student A: pretend to be one of the people on your chart. Describe yourself to Student B. Student B: make suggestions for somewhere for Student A to stay. Compare your suggestions. Then swap roles.

> **Useful language**
>
> **Making suggestions**
>
> What / How about + (verb + -ing) …?   Why don't you …?
> I suggest + (verb + -ing)   Perhaps you could …
> One idea / option is …   You could also consider … (verb + -ing)

4 Write a reply to one of these emails. Use the relevant information from exercises 2 and 3.

 EXAM TASK

You have received this email from your English-speaking friend, Susanna.

From: Susanna

Subject: Visit!

I'm going to be in your town in the autumn. I'm bringing my aunt and uncle. I'm sure you remember them, don't you? I have to leave early so they'll be on their own for a couple of days. Can you recommend some things for them to do? And do you know any good hotels?

Thanks,

Susanna

You have received this email from your English-speaking friend, Laura.

From: Laura

Subject: Need your help!

I'm in your town next week. I'm doing an IT training course with two new employees at the company. My boss has asked me to book somewhere to stay. She also wants me to think of something for us to do the next day. It's going to be difficult because I've never met them before! Can you give me any suggestions?

Look forward to hearing from you!

Laura

You have received this email from your English-speaking friend, Mo.

From: Mo

Subject: Guess what?

I'm coming to your town next week! I'm bringing my cousin. She's really looking forward to it! She's crazy about music and art. And going out, of course! Can you recommend some places where I can take her? And do you know anywhere not too expensive to stay?

Let me know if you're free and we can meet up too!

Cheers!

Mo

Exam tip!

When making suggestions or recommendations, always give your reasons for them.

What sort of camper are you?

1 Read the questionnaire and choose the best answers for you.

When you go camping ...

1 Where do you prefer to sleep?
  A under the stars
  B in a tent
  C in a bed
  D on a thin mattress

2 What do you like to eat?
  A whatever fruit, roots and insects you can find
  B hot dogs from a campfire
  C in a restaurant on-site
  D a bowl of pasta with all the family

3 Where do you hope to wash?
  A in the stream
  B in the campsite toilets
  C in a (small) bathroom
  D in your own bathroom

4 What do you like to bring with you?
  A just the clothes on your back
  B mosquito repellent, torch, wellies, spare pillow, saucepan, mugs, corn flakes and wipes
  C your best clothes
  D your favourite things from home

5 What do you answer to the question: 'Are you having a good time?'
  A 'I'm loving it!'
  B 'It's great to get away from it all.'
  C 'Of course. Why do you ask?'
  D 'Yes, but I didn't get much sleep because my best friend snores.'

Now check your answers.

*Your answers are **mainly A**. You like extreme camping. For you, camping is about going back to basics and forgetting that civilisation exists.*

*Your answers are **mainly B**. You like tent camping. For you, camping is and always will be about getting outdoors and getting away from it all for a week.*

*Your answers are **mainly C**. You like glamping. You like the idea of camping, but not the inconvenience. Life's too short to do without luxuries.*

*Your answers are **mainly D**. You love your camper van. You prefer to go camping with friends and you like the familiar comforts of home.*

2 Read the email below. Where in the email could you add the words in the box? You may be able to use them in more than one place.

> really   loads of   so   anyway   a bit   awesome

✉

Hi George

We're having a great time here at the campsite. We arrived at night, but luckily it only took three hours to put up the tent. We were tired when we woke up this morning and then we found we'd put up our tent in the campsite manager's garden. He was unhappy.

We all had chocolate biscuits and popcorn for breakfast this morning. Now we're off to the beach. It's good fun. We're all excited.

How are things? Why don't you join us? Send us a text when you're on your way and can you bring mosquito repellent?

Cheers!

Kai

---

3 **Answer the questions. What do you think?**

a) Does Kai know George well?

b) How would you describe the style of the email?

c) What effect does adding the phrases in exercise 2 have on the email?

4 **Read Tina's email to Jo.**

Dear Jo

I'm writing because I saw the information about your treehouse in Devon.

I'm a student from Manchester studying Environmental Science and I'm looking for somewhere unusual to stay for a month in the summer. Your treehouse looks perfect!

I'd like to know a little more about it. How many people can stay in the treehouse and is it safe to stay in if the weather is bad?

Would you be able to send me some photos of it? The one on the website is not very clear. Also, do you know of any wildlife groups who might be looking for volunteers in the summer?

Thanks in advance for your help. I look forward to hearing from you.

Best wishes

Tina Trent

> **Exam tip!**
>
> *In an email, think about who you are writing to, what you are writing about and which style would be appropriate.*

5 **Now choose the correct word in each sentence.**

a) Tina is writing to someone she *knows* / *doesn't know* well.

b) Tina is writing to someone who is *likely* / *not likely* to have similar interests.

c) Tina is writing about a *difficult* / *pleasant* matter.

d) The style of the email is *polite and formal* / *semi-formal* / *informal*.

6 **Read the exam task and write your email.**

✎ EXAM TASK

You see this notice in an English-language magazine:

> Like camping but don't like the rain? My log cabin on the edge of Northgate Forest combines everything you need for a comfortable stay with all the joys (and none of the disadvantages) of outdoor living.
>
> Contact melanie@fastmail.com for details on availability, prices and things to do in the area. Don't forget to tell me a bit about yourself.

Write your **email**.

'I look forward to your reply'

1 The email below is from an English-speaking boss to his new member of staff. Read the email and a sample reply. Is the style of the reply appropriate? Why / Why not?

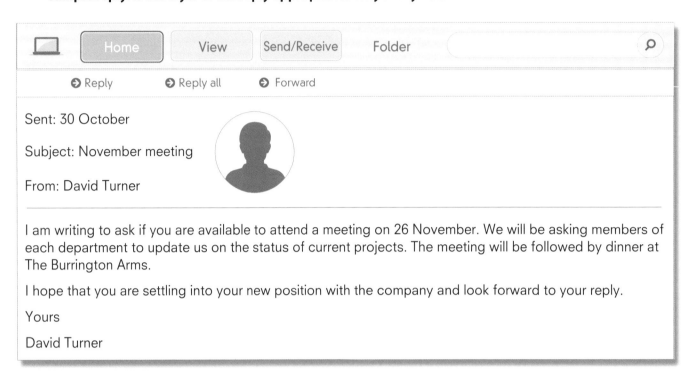

Sent: 30 October

Subject: November meeting

From: David Turner

I am writing to ask if you are available to attend a meeting on 26 November. We will be asking members of each department to update us on the status of current projects. The meeting will be followed by dinner at The Burrington Arms.

I hope that you are settling into your new position with the company and look forward to your reply.

Yours

David Turner

Dear David

Thanks for your email. Really sorry, but I can't make it. I've got another meeting on the same day! What a shame! I wanted to get to know everyone and I've heard good things about The Burrington Arms too!

Toni will be able to let the guys know how things are going. But do get in touch if I can be of any more help. Hope we can get together another time.

Love,

2 Put the sentences in order to write a reply with the same information but in a more formal style.

a) I look forward to seeing you again in the near future. ☐

b) Toni will be able to inform colleagues about current progress. ☐

c) Do contact me if I can be of any further assistance. ☐

d) It would have been a good opportunity to meet everyone and The Burrington Arms is highly recommended. ☐

e) Unfortunately I will not be able to attend as I have another meeting on the same day. ☐

f) Thank you for your email of 30 October. ☐

g) Kind regards, ☐

h) Please accept my apologies. ☐

3 **Choose the more formal option in the sentences.**

a) *I don't need / It won't be necessary* to leave early.

b) I *got / received* the *stuff / goods* yesterday.

c) Lewis is *making good progress / getting on well*.

d) I would like to *accept / take up* your offer.

e) Have you managed to *sort out / arrange* the travel?

f) We have considered *your request / what you asked for*.

g) I do not agree with *the things she did / her actions*.

h) There have been *loads / a large number* of complaints.

i) Could you please send me *further details / more info*?

4 **Which of the statements are true? Correct the false ones.**

a) Many common words and phrases in English have a more formal equivalent.   *True*

b) Phrasal verbs tend to be used in informal emails.

c) Phrases using 'get' are often used in formal emails.

d) Sentences in formal emails tend to be shorter.

e) Informal language used in a formal email gives a good impression.

f) There are fixed expressions you can learn which are often used in formal correspondence.

g) Exclamation marks are often used in formal emails.

h) Informal emails are usually sent between friends.

5 **Read the exam task and write your email.**

✏ EXAM TASK

You receive this email from a Japanese colleague, who works in the Tokyo branch of the same company.

International Business Now conference

 Tomiko Miyagi

I am writing to invite you to the International Business Now conference in Tokyo. We would be very pleased if you could attend our presentation on social conventions in Japan. The conference starts at 8 am on 4 April. We will be able to meet you at the airport on that day. You are very welcome to bring a colleague with you if you would like.

I look forward to your reply.

Yours sincerely,

Tomiko

Write your **email**.

> **Exam tip!**
>
> *Before writing an email, consider whether the situation requires formal or informal style.*

'Yours sincerely'

1 Look at the advert below. In which departments does this theme park have jobs available?

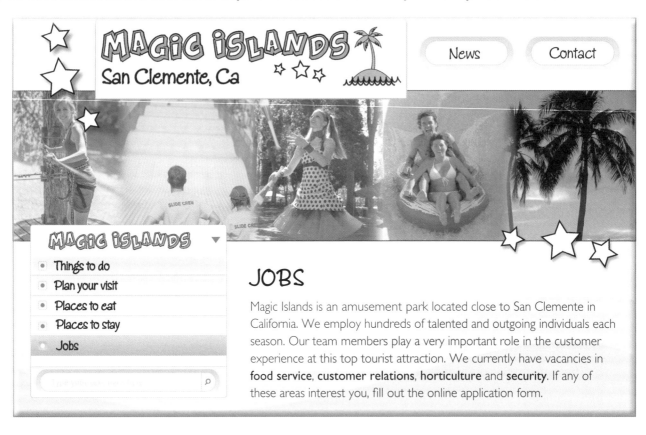

2 Discuss with a partner. Which of these skills are most important for the four different vacancies at this theme park?

- have good communication skills
- have self-confidence
- be knowledgeable about plants
- be trustworthy
- be organised

- be a team player
- have a reasonable level of physical fitness
- be willing to learn
- be quick-thinking
- be able to work under pressure

3 Look at the guidelines for writing a formal email and then read Ethan's formal email request. Which of the guidelines does he follow?

Guidelines for writing a formal email

- ☐ Use a neutral email address.
- ☐ Use a short and accurate subject header.
- ☐ Introduce yourself and/or your reason for writing in the first paragraph.
- ☐ Express your ideas politely.
- ☐ Avoid informal language.
- ☐ Avoid contractions. (e.g. I'd)
- ☐ Sign with your full name.

Sent: 19th May

Subject: letter of recommendation

From: ethan.funnyguy@webmail.ca

To: enquiries@eastsideschool.ca.org

I am writing to request a letter of recommendation in support of my application for a position in food service at Magic Islands theme park.

Magic Islands is currently seeking restaurant crew members. I would be responsible for preparing meal orders accurately and quickly, providing friendly customer service and working as part of a team.

As a student at Eastside School, I enjoyed Food Tech classes and believe I was organised and polite. I would be grateful if you could email a brief letter to <u>a.sanchez@diamondsprings.com</u>, outlining my suitability for the posts.

Thank you in advance for your assistance.

Yours sincerely

Ethan Moore

4a **Which form of leave-taking does Ethan use? Which of these other forms could he use in a formal email?**

> Best wishes / Lots of love / Regards / Yours / Love / Yours faithfully
>
> Let me know. / Hope to hear from you soon. / I look forward to hearing from you.

4b **Which of the phrases in the box is the most informal?**

5 **Ethan doesn't use a salutation as he is sending this email to a general email address. Which of these could he use in a formal email? Which of these are the most informal?**

> Dear Sir/Madam / Hi Joe / Dear Mr Reed / Hello there / Dear Joe / Hi guys / Dear Sir / Dear Madam

6 **How would the guidelines in exercise 3 be different if Ethan was writing a formal letter (rather than an email)?**

7 **Read the exam task and write your email.**

 EXAM TASK

You see this advertisement on the noticeboard of your English-language school:

> Diamond Springs Water and Theme Park is hiring individuals aged 16 and over to fill a variety of positions in the departments listed: food service, gift shop, ride operators, water safety. If you would like to have more information on our vacancies and working conditions, direct your emails to vacancies@ diamondsprings.com, indicating briefly which department you would be interested in and your suitability.

Write your **email**.

In character

1   To help you think of ideas for a story, try creating a strong character. Answer these questions using the suggestions to help you.

(1) What is your character's name?

(2) How does your character walk?

> creep   dash   march   plod   skip   stride   stroll   tiptoe   wander

(3) How does your character speak?

> bravely   calmly   cheerfully   excitedly   in a loud voice
> in a whisper   jokingly   kindly   politely   proudly   rudely   wisely

(4) How does your character look at other people?

> examine   gaze   glance   glare   peep   peer   stare

(5) What are the key features of your character?

> a beard   bald   broad shoulders   bushy eyebrows   dark-skinned   fair-skinned
> in her early twenties   long eyelashes   middle-aged   of average height
> overweight   spots   stocky   wiry   wrinkles

(6) Does your character do any of these?

> bite his/her bottom lip   fold his/her arms   have bitten fingernails
> laugh loudly   look down at the ground   play with his/her hair
> scratch his/her chin/head/nose   smile broadly   tap his/her foot

(7) Does your character have an interest or passion or something he/she hates?

(8) Who does your character live with?

2   Think about these situations. What would your character do in these situations?

a) They meet a new person.

b) They walk into an empty hallway.

c) They lose their phone.

d) They see a robbery.

e) They are outside when a bad storm starts.

f) They discover a secret room in a house.

3a A story has a beginning, a middle and an end. Choose one of these opening lines from a story. Write the name of your character in the gap.

As the taxi drove away, ... realised the bag was still on the seat.

.... walked into the room and knew immediately that there was something missing.

.... laughed as soon as he/she saw the tickets.

.... ran as fast as he/she could to the boat.

3b Think of an ending for the story. Make notes about the events that lead up to this. Your story must include: an argument and a door key.

> **Exam tip!**
>
> *In the story task of the First exam, you will not be asked to write a description of a character, but having a strong character in mind can help you to come up with ideas for a story.*

4 Look at the exam task. Create a character for your story, think of an ending and make notes about the storyline.

....

....

....

✎ **EXAM TASK**

You have seen this announcement in an international magazine for young people.

> **Stories wanted**
>
> We are looking for stories for our new English-language magazine for young people.
>
> Your story must **begin** with this sentence:
>
> *Lena walked into the hotel and looked around anxiously.*
>
> ● a meeting
> ● a text message

5 Write your story.

6 Compare your stories in pairs. Are the stories or characters similar in any way?

> **Exam tip!**
>
> *Adding a couple of lines of dialogue will add interest to your story.*

A discovery and a map

1a   **Work in pairs. Describe the buildings. Use the words in the box to help you.**

> apartment   block / block of flats   brick   concrete   in good/bad condition   detached   high-rise
>
> isolated   neglected   ordinary   ruined   run-down   shabby   stone   terraced   typical   well-situated

1b   **Which of the words in exercise 1a are adjectives?**

2   **Imagine you are inside one of the buildings. Use the words in the box to help you answer the questions.**

> bright   clean   comfortable   cramped   damp   dusty   modern   modest   spacious

a)   What can you see?

b)   How does it smell?

c)   How does it make you feel?

✎ EXAM TASK

You have seen this announcement in an international magazine for young people.

Stories wanted

We are looking for stories for our new English-language magazine for young people.

Your story must **begin** with this sentence:

The house was not as Evan had imagined.

Your story must include:

- a discovery
- a map

---

3   **Read the exam task. Answer the questions to create a setting and build a storyline.**

a)   Where is the house?

b)   What does the house look like?

c)   How does Evan feel in the house?

d)   Why is Evan there?

e)   What discovery does Evan make?

f)   Why does Evan have a map?

g)   How does the story end?

4   **Write your story.**

PHOTOCOPIABLE

Recommending a book

1 Think about a book you have read recently. Did you enjoy it? Why / Why not? Discuss with a partner. Have they read the same book?

2 Complete the sentences with the words from the box.

> cliffhanger plot villain relationship setting theme

a) The .... is an evil character in a story.

b) The .... of a film is the main subject or idea.

c) The place or time where the events in a book happen are the ....

d) When you are left to wonder what will happen at the end of a book or film, it is called a ....

e) The way two characters behave towards each other or the feelings they have for one another can be described as their ....

f) The main events in a story make up the ....

3 These are questions from a set text exam task. Match the two parts of the questions.

1 Describe an important event in the book

2 In what ways is the setting

3 Describe how an unexpected moment in the book

4 Did you like the ending of the story

5 Describe a scene in the story which you found

6 Imagine that you are the hero/heroine of the story for one day

7 Describe a villain from the story

8 Who is the most interesting

9 What are the main

10 How does the relationship between the characters

a) significant to the story?

b) and say why he/she is bad.

c) frightening, exciting or amusing

d) or can you think of another way it could have finished?

e) character in the book and why?

f) made you feel.

g) and say how it affects the rest of the story.

h) themes of the story?

i) change during the book?

j) and describe what happens to you.

4 Which of the above questions would be appropriate to ask about the book you discussed in exercise 1? Tell your partner and explain why.

5 Read the exam task and write your email.

> **Exam tip!**
>
> *Remember that the set text question is optional so DO NOT attempt to answer this question if you haven't read the book or seen the film!*

6 ✎ **EXAM TASK**

> You receive an email from your friend asking you to recommend a book with interesting characters. Write your email based on the set text.

Part 1

You **must** answer this question. Write your answer in **140–190** words in an appropriate style.

1   In your English class, you have been talking about different ways to study. Now your English teacher has asked you to write an essay for homework.

Write your essay using **all** the notes and giving reasons for your point of view.

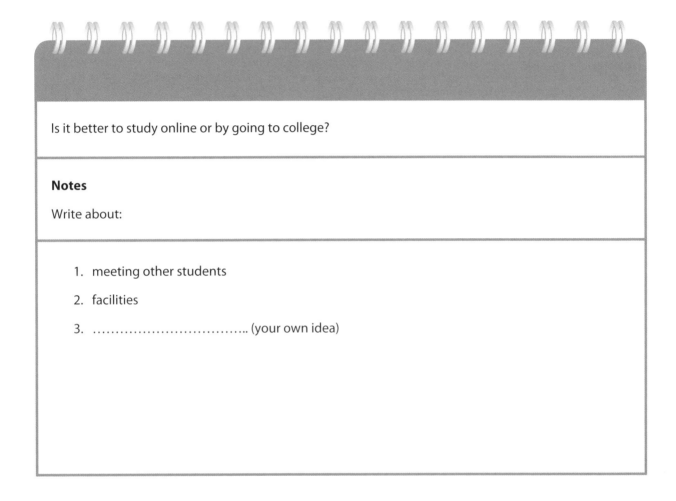

Is it better to study online or by going to college?

Notes

Write about:

1. meeting other students
2. facilities
3. …………………………….. (your own idea)

PHOTOCOPIABLE

Part 2

Write an answer to **one** of the questions **2–4** in this part. Write your answer in **140–190** words in an appropriate style.

---

2   You see this announcement in your college English-language magazine.

> **Articles wanted**
>
> **Who can save the planet?**
>
> Climate change affects us all. But is it up to the factories and the governments of the world to put it right? Or are there things we can do right now which will help to make the difference? Write an article telling us your views.
>
> The best articles will be published in our magazine.

Write your **article**.

3   You have received this email from a local sports teacher, Mr Hunting.

> **From:** Magnus Hunting
>
> **Subject:** Running club
>
> I'm thinking of starting up a running club in this area. Do you think people would be interested? How often should I ask people to come? Have you got any other suggestions?
>
> Magnus

Write your **email**.

4   You see this announcement on an English-language school website.

> Your local council is looking into ways of reducing traffic congestion in your area.
>
> You have been asked to write a report for the local councillor. Your report should:
>
> • include information about the traffic problems that people in your area have to deal with
>
> • recommend possible solutions and why they would be successful

Write your **report**.

Part 1

You **must** answer this question. Write your answer in **140–190** words in an appropriate style.

1   In your English class, you have been talking about healthy lifestyles. Now your English teacher has asked you to write an essay for homework.

Write your essay using **all** the notes and giving reasons for your point of view.

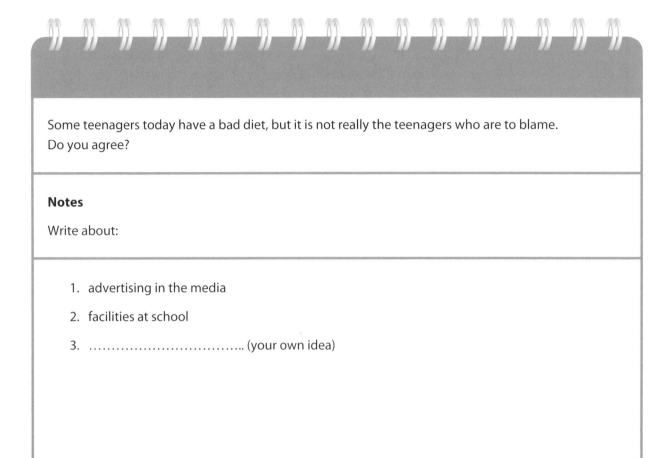

Some teenagers today have a bad diet, but it is not really the teenagers who are to blame.
Do you agree?

Notes

Write about:

1. advertising in the media

2. facilities at school

3. …………………………….. (your own idea)

Part 2

Write an answer to one of the questions **2–4** in this part. Write your answer in **140–190** words in an appropriate style.

2   You have received this email from your English-speaking friend, Rajeev.

> I haven't heard from you for a long time. I hope you are OK. We're doing a project in class about school clubs. Do you take part in any clubs at school? Would you recommend the club? And what advice do you have for someone wanting to join?
>
> Thanks for your help!
>
> Rajeev

Write your **email**.

3   You see this announcement in an English-language magazine for schools.

> **Reviews wanted**
>
> ## Technology you can't live without!
>
> We're doing an article on the technology you love most. What is your favourite device? Why do you like it so much? Tell us why you think other people your age should own one.
>
> We will publish the best reviews next month.

Write your **review**.

4   You see this notice on an English-Language school website.

> ## Stories wanted
>
> Can you write a good story? We want to find the best new storywriters out there.
>
> Your story must **begin** with this sentence:
>
> *From the moment Kerry woke up, she knew it was going to be a different kind of day.*
>
> Your story must include:
>
> • a phone number
>
> • a surprise

Write your **story**.

5   Your English class has had a discussion about the set text. Now your teacher has given you this essay for homework:

In the set text, what do you think is the most important event in the story, and why?

Write your **essay**.

Answers

Great work (pages 6–7)

1 1b 2d 3a 4c 5e

3 **Sample answers**

In my country, being a lawyer is well-respected. As a result many students want to become a lawyer after their studies.

In my opinion, nurses are undervalued. It must be very difficult to care for patients and work such long hours.

4 **1** Giving your opinion **2** Justifying your opinion

5 **Sample answer**

Sportspeople work very hard and deserve good salaries. However, there are people in other professions who also work hard and should also be valued more.

Some professional sportspeople, such as footballers, earn very large amounts of money. One reason for this is that becoming a successful sportsperson requires years of dedication and training. They train hard every day and in all weathers. In my opinion, they give a lot of satisfaction and inspiration to many people. Watching the success of a national sportsperson or a sports team can bring people together.

On the other hand, there are other people who also work very hard and do not earn enough. Nurses in my country are underpaid, but we could not live without them. Lifeboat crew save many lives every year and work in dangerous conditions. In my view, they should be well paid, but most of them are voluntary.

As far as I am concerned, it is unfair that sportspeople earn more than other dedicated workers. It is a sign of inequality in our society.

Transport going forward (pages 8–9)

1 **a)** traffic congestion **e)** cycle paths
b) urban areas **f)** fossil fuels
c) means of transport **g)** rechargeable batteries
d) rush hour **h)** carbon emissions / zero emissions

4 b

5 a

6 **Sample answer**

In today's world, we are all very aware of the need to find alternatives to using petrol. Electric cars are definitely a step forward but there are also a number of disadvantages to owning one.

There is no doubt that electric cars are better for the environment. They produce zero emissions and they consume relatively little electricity. Electric cars are also quiet and will therefore make a difference to noise pollution in cities.

However, we should remember that most electricity is still produced by burning fossil fuels. Electric cars do not solve the controversial issue of what to do about fossil fuels and the damage they cause to the environment. Furthermore, the technology in electric cars is new and is likely to be expensive and not very efficient. Being quiet can also be a disadvantage as numbers of pedestrians involved in road accidents may increase.

To conclude, electric cars are a great invention but research still needs to be done into forms of transport that are even more eco-friendly.

A meat-free future (pages 10–11)

1 Is a meat-free diet the only healthy diet?

2 The writer mentions **a** and **d.**

3 **a)** in moderation **b)** diabetes **c)** preservatives
d) livestock **e)** ethical **f)** protein

4 The correct answer is **b)**. Conclusion **a)** contradicts the information in the essay. A new idea is suddenly introduced in conclusion **c)**.

5a To conclude In my opinion For all these reasons, I firmly believe

5b *In conclusion, To summarise* and *To sum up* could be used instead of *To conclude.*

On balance and *All in all* could be used in place of *For all these reasons.*

As far as I'm concerned has a similar meaning to *In my opinion.*

6 **Sample answer**

Vegetarianism is a choice that many people make for ethical reasons. In today's world, though, there are other important reasons for a meat-free diet.

There are some well-known health risks associated with eating red meat, such as high blood pressure and heart disease. We should also not ignore that chemical preservatives are often added to meat or to the animal feed, and these may also affect our health in the long-term.

We all know that levels of CO_2 in our atmosphere are too high. However, one of the most harmful greenhouse gases is methane. Methane is produced by intensive livestock farming. For this reason, meat production actually contributes to pollution.

A meat-free diet is not an easy option. It can be difficult to obtain iron and zinc from a vegetarian diet. However, vegetarian food is often fresh, full of vitamins and inexpensive. We should all make more effort to eat less meat, even if it's only one or two times a week.

To sum up, a meat-free diet is something we should all consider for health reasons, but also if we are serious about looking after our environment.

Too young for Facebook? (pages 12–13)

3

✔	✘
1 bullying isn't caused by social media sites	1 kids don't realise how what they say affects others
2 a life skill	2 too many emotional pressures
3 they are already using it	3 they're lying to get on there

4   **a)** They don't get how what they say truly affects others.
b) It can stress them out.
c) We want this kid to grow up truthful, right?
d) We all have to take notice of this.
e) What's so great about Facebook? There's loads of games he can play … and supervised networking sites …
f) Using social media is something they've got to learn.

5   **Sample answers**
a) More and more children these days are going onto social media sites under the age of thirteen.
b) The main reason for this is peer pressure and wanting to keep up with older siblings.
c) Generally, knowledge of social media sites is an essential life skill, but not until you are ready to use them.

6   **Sample answer**
More and more children are going on social media sites under the age of thirteen. As responsible members of society, we should not ignore this issue because it concerns us all.

Learning how to use social media is definitely an essential life skill. In the future children are going to be interacting online with friends, and with business colleagues too. This is a skill they need to grow up with. In fact, it is almost impossible to stop them.

By allowing younger members of our society to join social media sites, we may be increasing the risk of bullying. What's more, it can be difficult to cope with the pressures of social media. Even some adults feel inadequate if they don't get many followers, for example.

There are a lot of ways for children to enjoy the Internet, such as games and supervised sites. We should encourage them to make the most of these and leave social media for later.

Digital generation (pages 14–15)

2   **a)** 3 **b)** This view is not expressed. **c)** 4 **d)** 1 **e)** 2 **f)** 5

3   **Sample answers**
a) They can record moments, relive them and share them with friends.
Everyone knows that virtual reality is not everyday life.
b) Young people still go out to meet friends and join clubs.
People today are talking to more people than ever before.
c) Technology helps them find topics to talk about.
Social media helps us meet a wide range of people.
d) We can be in touch with more people than ever before.
People use texts to arrange to meet up.
e) It's easy to call or contact them.
People discuss texts they have received and sites they have looked up.
f) Young people love having the power to get in touch with people and find out information whenever they want.
They can organise their lives more quickly and easily online.

4   **Sample answers**
a) On the one hand, you could say that young people have forgotten how to enjoy the moment. On the other hand, they can relive the moment on their mobiles and share it with friends.

b) There is no doubt that young people can lose themselves in a virtual reality which is much more exciting than everyday life. However, arranging to go out with friends and finding out what's on has never been easier.

c) Social media gives young people the option to meet only people they like. In spite of this, they are meeting more people than ever before. What's more, some of these people are from cultures they could not have got to know otherwise.

5   Phrases used to express contrasting points of view: *On the one hand, On the other hand, However, In spite of this.* Phrase used to provide an additional point of view: *There is no doubt that, What's more.*

6   **a)** A **b)** C **c)** A **d)** C **e)** C **f)** A **g)** C

7 Sample plan

Paragraphs	Content notes	Useful phrases
Introduction (give examples of the digital generation)	digital generation not like any before.	more access to technology socialise, chat, arrange dates
First point of view and opposing point of view	meet people with same likes chat with people from other cultures	Some say … However,
Second point of view and opposing point of view	forgotten how to live in the moment replay send to others	too busy recording it In fact, What's more
Third point of view and opposing point of view	prefer to text than speak arrange to meet by text	It is true … though
Conclusion: stating your final point of view	only communicate with their screens? reach out more	On the one hand On the other hand youth of today keep in constant touch

8 Sample answer

Young people today are the digital generation. This generation has more access to technology than any generation before them. They use technology to chat, socialise and arrange dates.

On social media sites, it is easy to meet people who have the same likes. Some people say that teenagers are not getting to know people with different beliefs. However, through the same sites it is also possible to chat with people from other cultures that they would not meet otherwise.

Some people say that teenagers have forgotten how to live in the moment. They are too busy recording it. In fact, they replay that moment. What's more, they send it to others so that they can experience it too.

It is true that many young people prefer to text instead of speak on the phone. They see their friends more often, though, because they arrange to meet them by text too.

You could say that young people only communicate with their screens. On the other hand, it is also true that they reach out to more people. This generation keeps in constant touch with others and with the world around them.

Criminal activity (pages 16–17)

1   THEFT

   1-3 break in (v), smuggle (v), steal (v)   **4-6** burglary (n), personal identity (n), robbery (n)

PRISON

1&2 be charged with (v), reoffend (v)   **3&4** convict (n/v), sentence (n/v)   **5** court (n)   **6** behind bars (phrase)
2 a) 13 million   **b)** 15% **c)** three months   **d)** ten minutes
e) £65,000   **f)** £50,000

3   **a)** There has been *a steady decrease* in burglaries. (*A drop* is a sudden change so it would not collocate with *steady*. You could talk about *a sudden drop*.)
   b) There has been *a sudden increase* in rates of cyber crime.
   c) Rates of personal identity theft have *risen / increased* dramatically.
   d) Car crimes *have dropped / have fallen / have decreased* by 15%.

4   Most people in the UK and USA now use the amazing qualities of the Internet on a daily basis, but unfortunately the Internet has also managed to create a new problem: cyber crime. There must be only a minority of households which have not been affected by some kind of cyber crime. Law enforcement agencies worldwide are trying to tackle the problem, but cyber crime is becoming more common and a considerable number of people have become victims of hacking, theft, identity theft and malicious software. All households should make sure they have the latest anti-virus and security software on their home systems, but even this is not infallible.

5   Sample answer

In my country the number of people in prison has doubled over recent years. This has encouraged the authorities to look for new and different ways to punish criminals, such as giving fines and community service.

Many people argue that those who have broken the law should be put in prison. Taking away their freedom will make them think about their actions. However, prisons are crowded and for this reason criminals do not always stay in prison for their whole sentence.

In the UK, around 60% of prisoners reoffend, compared with about a third of people who do community service. Community service allows people to integrate better into society and it often includes some form of education.

Lastly there is the question of cost. It is extremely expensive to look after someone in prison. The cost to the taxpayer of community service is a lot less.

All in all, neither system is perfect but community service seems to have a better success rate for people who commit small crimes. Consequently, I believe we should extend and improve the system of community service.

Celebrity status (pages 18–19)

1   Suggested answers

a) readers in their late teens or early 20s

b) informal and fun

4   Sample answers

Two points in favour of a celeb lifestyle:

1 parties and meeting other famous people

2 money

Further ideas, opinions or examples:

places you can only dream of going; seeing actors you admire

money isn't everything, but it does help

Two points in favour of enjoying life the way it is:

1 being able to go out and not worry what I look like

2 not having to worry about the paparazzi

Further ideas, opinions or examples:

I like to take the dog for a walk in the morning with my old clothes on. It's my time.

Media stories about celebs who want to stop paparazzi intruding on their private lives, e.g. the British Royal Family

Conclusion: *When I weigh it all up … be happy with what you have.*

5   Sample answer

There are times when I look at photos of celebrities on this website and I wish I could be them. I'd like to share the glamour, the excitement, the cameras … or would I?

There's no doubt celebs can go to parties I can only dream of. I'm a big fan of Johnny Depp. Imagine walking into a party and seeing him there! Of course, the money would be nice too. Money isn't everything, but it helps. Holiday anyone? Next week? Great! I'm coming.

But when I stop to think about it, I'm not so sure. I love my weekends. It makes a change not to worry what I look like. I put on my old clothes and take the dog for a walk. It's my time. I really wouldn't like someone to be there with a camera. You read in the media about famous people, like the British royal family, who have to work really hard to stop the paparazzi from intruding on their private lives.

When I weigh it all up, there's only one answer. I am happy with what I have. Even the old clothes.

Taking a gap year (pages 20–21)

1   The people chose to: volunteer to help schoolchildren in Ghana, get some work experience locally, volunteer in sea turtle conservation in Mexico, go on a language course and take a work placement in Italy.

Benefits they mention: preparation for living away from home, confidence to try new things and learn from experience, motivation for further studies, learning about another culture, have amazing experiences, become more independent and assertive, have a better CV.

2   Suggested answers

1 Make a plan for when you get back. Apply to college or get in touch with an employer before you go.

2 Make sure you know why you are taking a gap year and organise what you are going to do before your year starts.

3 Once you have made your plan, talk it through with someone else.

4 If you are going on an organised gap year programme, speak to at least one past participant. Don't just read what's on the website!

5 Get to know the local people and their culture. Enjoy yourself!

3 & 4

1 b) is more appropriate. Asking questions is one way to make your writing more engaging.

2 a) The writer is addressing the reader directly.

3 a) Shorter sentences are more likely to keep the reader's attention.

4 b) Include personal examples in an article.

5 b) Use some idioms and multi-word verbs to make your writing more informal and interesting.

4   Sample answer

So there's only one topic of conversation at college right now. What are you going to do next? And for some, should I take a gap year?

I remember how worried I felt. A year with no studies seemed like a long time. My teacher told me to make a list of all the things I'd like to learn. Then I looked up gap year programmes to see which I could really do. I soon came up with a short list of two or three.

Worried about money? You're right to be. Gap years can be expensive. But start saving now and you'll be surprised how it adds up. And don't forget you can work during your gap year too.

The big one was my parents. They thought I was just wasting time. But I knew that they wanted me to succeed. I told them what I wanted to learn during my year and they soon understood.

A gap year is just one year of your life. But if you get yourself organised, it could be one of the best.

Why here? Why now? (pages 22–23)

2   The writer needs to explain why they decided to take an English course at this time and in this place.

4

	Text A	Text B
STYLE		
Is it the right style for an article? Why / Why not?	It's a good style overall. But first of all and secondly would be more appropriate in the essay task.	It's not appropriate. The style is too serious for an article. Try having more fun with the style!
ANSWERING THE QUESTION		
Does the article answer the key points in the question?	Yes, it does.	Yes, it does.
Are all the points relevant?	The final paragraph is not relevant to the exam task.	Yes.
Is it about the right length?	No, it's too short. Try adding more detail.	Yes, just right.
LANGUAGE		
Give examples of good vocabulary the writer has used.	section manager, bankrupt, quit	cultural, economic, business reasons, negotiating
Has the writer used a variety of structures?	It's quite simple. Try not to overuse the structure *make + me + adjective*. Check the use of 'told'.	You've tried to include some more complex structures. Well done!
Give examples of any spelling or grammar you would correct.	No spelling mistakes! ~~It made me surprise.~~ It surprised me. ~~I am interested in British music very much.~~ I am very interested in British music. ~~which makes me satisfied very much~~ which is very satisfying.	~~citys~~ cities, ~~to~~ two, ~~felled~~ felt, ~~europe~~ Europe, ~~client's~~ clients, the more I see the city (~~the more I saw~~)

6 **Sample answer**

Last year I quit my job and came to study English here in Queenstown, New Zealand. But why now? And why here?

Quitting my job was a big decision and my friends were really concerned. But with good English I can get a better job in the future. Imagine a job interview where there are two excellent applicants, but only one of them speaks good English. Guess which one gets the job? A lot of the internet sites I access are in English now so it's an essential skill.

I love adventure sports and New Zealand is the perfect

place to do them. Since arriving, I've already been zip-lining and travelled down the Shotover River by jet boat! Queenstown is small so there is plenty of opportunity to get to know the friendly people. Meeting the other language students is amazing too. It's truly international here. I've met people from South East Asia, Japan and India.

New Zealand is a great place to learn English and I'm having the time of my life. I'll remember it forever when I go back home. If I go home …

Take sleep seriously! (pages 24–25)

2 **Suggested answer**

The article is confusing and difficult to read because there are no paragraphs.

3 **Introduction**: Research suggests that many teenagers are getting just five hours of sleep a night. Teachers report teenagers falling asleep in class and many keep their energy levels up with sugary drinks and snacks. But it's not just teenagers. The recommended number of hours of sleep for adults is 7 to 9, yet a survey conducted by the National Sleep Foundation in the US found 39% of people in the UK and 66% of Japanese people slept for less than 7 hours on work nights.

Paragraph 1: The cortex – the part of the brain which controls thinking, speech and memory – needs time off at the end of the day. Without sleep, we become forgetful, less able to maintain conversations and find it harder to concentrate. Long-term sleep loss makes us more vulnerable to illness and mood swings. A study of the sleeping habits of 12 to 18 year olds shows that those that sleep less than five hours a night are 70% more likely to suffer depression. So why do we do it?

Paragraph 2: In today's society we are constantly pushing ourselves to achieve more, and cutting into our sleeping time is inevitable. Many of us are using our smartphones way into the night to keep in touch, keep up-to-date and not miss out. Stimulants like caffeine and sugar are delaying our sleep at night.

Paragraph 3: Believe it or not, there's now a thing called sleep-training. And their advice is: get some exercise during the day and don't nap in the afternoon. Eat a full meal in the early evening and avoid eating chocolate or drinking coffee before bed. Don't text, use a computer or watch TV for half an hour before going to bed and sleep somewhere which is not too warm and not too bright.

Conclusion: In short, it's time we started to look after ourselves and take sleep seriously.

4 **Sample plan**

Introduction: Lots of people don't get enough sleep. But for me a good night's sleep is the most important thing.

Paragraph 1: How many hours sleep do you get? How does it make you feel?

Paragraph 2: Why is a good sleep important?

Paragraph 3: What are your tips for a good night's sleep?

Conclusion: In a world where are minds are constantly busy (social media, etc.), sleep is more important than ever.

6 Sample answer

'I was up so late last night!' Lots of people I know don't get enough sleep. But, if you ask me, a good sleep is the most important thing.

I've read articles about getting eight hours of sleep, but surely it's not the number of hours, it's the quality. I aim for seven hours of well-earned rest. In the morning, I'm ready for anything. Even if I have a stressful day ahead of me, I know I can cope.

A good night's sleep is important because it gives your body a chance to recharge its batteries. Your brain, which has been busy all day, needs a break. And your eyes? They get a rest from the glare of your tablet and phone screens.

Want to know my tips? There's only one. Turn off all your technology half an hour before you go to bed and relax. Have a warm drink if you want to or listen to some gentle music.

In a world where our minds are always on the go and always looking for information, sleep is more important than ever. That's why I always make sure I get mine.

Hallowe'en: A time to have fun (pages 26–27)

1 Suggested answers

b) Probably not. The style is quite neutral, too simple and a little boring.

2 Sample answer

Hallowe'en in America is one huge party. But to enjoy it you don't have to be a kid! Teenagers and adults love it too. In fact, everyone joins in.

Hallowe'en is the best holiday because it is such amazing fun. Dressing up is a great thing to do! So come to America for Hallowe'en! Have fun! And don't worry what the neighbours think!

3 Sample answer

Diwali is an ancient autumn festival celebrated all over the world by Hindus, Jains and Sikhs. The festival, which is about the victory of light over darkness and good over evil, is my favourite time of year.

Ask anyone in my family what they like best about Diwali and they'll say that it's the flickering lights and the glowing oil lamps. We place them all around the house and in the streets until everything looks magical! Each light represents hope.

Preparing for Diwali is the part I like the best. We start decorating the house for five to ten days before the event. We prepare delicious sweets, go shopping for gifts and get out our best clothes.

It wouldn't be Diwali without a party. Diwali is a time to meet up with friends and family, dance and eat, and what could be better than that? I'm sure you've heard the Diwali fireworks exploding in the autumn sky … so next time you hear them think of me!

Never give up (page 28)

1 'There's nothing like parkour. <u>It's had a big effect on me</u>. I've stopped smoking, my diet <u>has improved</u> and I <u>know more about</u> exercise now too. I'm a <u>friendlier</u> person, <u>definitely happier</u> and <u>more relaxed</u> … I've met so many new friends, people who have welcomed me with open arms. Even my relationship with my family is <u>much better</u>.

As a traceur, I try to follow the philosophy <u>as much as possible</u>. When I train <u>harder</u>, my everyday outlook changes. Any obstacle can be overcome. Never give up. Pace yourself and gradually you will be able to push your limits <u>even further</u>.'

2 'There's nothing like parkour. It's <u>changed me a lot</u>. I've stopped smoking, my diet <u>has got healthier</u> and I <u>have a greater understanding of</u> exercise now too. I'm a <u>more amiable</u> person, <u>certainly more cheerful</u> and <u>more easy-going</u> … I've met so many new friends, people who have welcomed me with open arms. Even my relationship with my family is <u>far better</u>.

As a traceur, I try to follow the philosophy <u>as much as I can</u>. When I train <u>more intensely</u>, my everyday outlook changes. Any obstacle can be overcome. Never give up. Pace yourself and gradually you will be able to push my limits <u>more and more</u>.'

3 Sample answer

Pilates is an exercise system which is quite similar to yoga. It was invented by Joseph Pilates and was originally used by dancers to help them become stronger.

I started going to Pilates classes a year ago. At first, I thought the classes would be easy, but I was definitely surprised! You need a lot of strength and control to do the exercises well. I soon found that, even on a busy day, I felt calmer after my Pilates class and I was sleeping much better too. After several months, I felt healthier and it even inspired me to make changes to my diet, such as cutting down on sugar.

Pilates is great because it means you can take a break from your busy routine and spend some time on yourself. We do breathing exercises in class and I try to practise these as often as I can. Another good thing is meeting up with new people who share your interest.

All exercise is good for you, but I can highly recommend Pilates if you like something calm and controlled. Why don't you give it a try?

Learning something new (page 29)

3   Sample answers

a) most of the trainees looked confused.

b) one trainee fell asleep!

c) we didn't receive any hand-outs.

d) I do not think it was good value for money.

e) I would not recommend this course to others.

5   Sample answer

Introduction
The purpose of this report is to review the recent first-aid training course attended by myself and my colleagues and to recommend whether the company arrange any more first-aid courses in future.

Pace of the course
The course was quite fast-paced. There were a lot of subjects to cover. As a result, there was not very much time to ask questions.

Hands-on practice
There were not many opportunities to practise what the leaders were telling us. Most of us had the opportunity to put a bandage on a colleague, but we did not practise basic life-saving skills, for example.

Trainers
Due to the fact that the trainers were young and inexperienced, they found it hard to explain first aid to us. Many of us on the course had no previous experience in first aid.

Conclusion
First-aid training is an essential skill at work and we were all motivated to learn. However, unfortunately none of my colleagues felt we learned very much on the course. For this reason, I would recommend arranging another first-aid course, but not with this particular company.

A vibrant city (pages 30–31)

3   Suggested answers

Historical city: Many of the important building in the city are from Victorian times.

Near countryside: Leeds is near three national parks.

Good nightlife: There are many nightclubs and venues in the city.

Close to an airport: Leeds has its own international airport.

A choice of language schools: There are a number of language schools in Leeds.

Well-connected by rail: Leeds is one hour from Manchester and two hours from London by train.

Wide range of shops: Leeds has been voted the best place to shop in the whole of the UK.

4   Suggested answers

a) It has its own international airport.

b) there is a lot of traffic

c) this means they can offer a more personal approach to learning

d) Leeds is a big city

e) there are some places, such as Chapel Town or Harehills, that are not recommended for visitors

6   Sample answer

To:
From:
Subject: Salamanca, Spain

Introduction
As requested, this report looks at the suitability of Salamanca as a site for a new language school.

Town centre and amenities
Salamanca is a small town, but because it is a university town, there are plenty of free-time activities for young people to do. The majority of people are aged between eighteen and thirty, and the nightlife, restaurants, bars and shops all welcome students.

Language schools and student life
Salamanca is the home of the oldest university in Spain and has a long tradition of student life. Spanish language courses are also offered at the university and often fully booked.

Cost of living
Many tourists come to Salamanca to see the historical buildings and the city is also close to Madrid. As a result, it is quite an expensive town to live in and rents for buildings can be high.

Conclusion
Salamanca is an excellent place to study Spanish. However, it is also quite expensive and there is likely to be a lot of competition from other language schools. For these reasons, I do not consider it suitable as a site for a new language school.

An eco-friendly home (pages 32–33)

2   a) 7 **b)** 6 **c)** 1 **d)** 4 **e)** 3 **f)** 2 **g)** 9 **h)** 5 **i)** 8

3 **a)** solar panels **b)** food waste bins **c)** outdoor lights **d)** green roofs **e)** micro wind turbines

4 **Sample answers**

In general, green roofs make as significant difference to the local surroundings.

I would definitely recommend that more information is given to residents about these.

Generally, double glazing is an easy and affordable solution to heating costs.

I would therefore recommend that residents install this in their homes.

5 **Sample answer**

Introduction

The aim of this report is to look at ways of making buildings and gardens in the local area more environmentally-friendly.

Solar panels

Solar panels can produce enough electricity for the owner's needs. In spite of being expensive to install, the owner will get their money back after only ten years. However, they require a lot of space on the roof or in the garden.

Native plants and trees

Residents can be encouraged to plant native plants to attract native insects. Trees, such as oak trees, are useful for attracting birds, especially if several are planted in the area.

Food waste bins

The council could be encouraged to provide food waste bins to reduce the amount of food waste in landfill sites. This waste produces methane.

Conclusion

On the whole, the suggestions above are easy to do. The more expensive suggestions are worthwhile in the long term. I believe that if the above recommendations were accepted, the local area would be greatly improved for the environment and for local residents.

The next best thing (pages 34–35)

1 **A (2)** is put on **(3)** charges up **(4)** is connected
B (1) is placed **(2)** is cut **(3)** go down **(4)** are eaten
C (1) are inserted **(2)** is shredded **(3)** (is) dissolved **(4)** is produced
D (1) floats **(2)** is powered **(3)** to be plugged in **(4)** require

3 **Sample answer**

Introduction

As requested, this report looks at three ideas for new inventions which have recently been submitted to the company and recommends which product the company should sell.

The dance-powered phone charger

This is an exciting invention which young people would enjoy and another good selling-point is that it is environmentally-friendly. However, at present, the product requires a lot of dancing in order to charge the phone.

The instant bird feeder

This product is very clever. The bread is placed on the cutting board and then the crumbs go down the tube and are eaten by birds. It is another eco-friendly invention but it could be easy for customers to make one of their own at home.

The Pool PC

This product would appeal to wealthy consumers who have their own swimming pool. The product is useful and it would be possible to sell it at quite a high price. The product is well-designed and has been tested by consumers.

Conclusion

There are good points about all of these products, but I would recommend the Pool PC as this is an attractive product which should be very popular.

A must-see film (pages 36–37)

2 The review on the right is for the novel *Q&A*. The review on the left is for the film *Slumdog Millionaire*.

3 **a)** a child with no parents **b)** gave the director the idea for the film **c)** new and different **d)** worth remembering **e)** understanding of **f)** make you have sympathy for **g)** complicated **h)** stunning **i)** you can believe this character exists

4 best-selling, original, fast-moving, memorable, good, bad, beautiful, shocking, believable, complicated, fast-paced, colourful, dazzling
The reviewer prefers the film.

5 **FB:** It's about …, It takes place in …, It is set in …, It is based on …, It tells the story of …, It's full of wonderful / stereotypical / comic characters, It has an unexpected / a predictable ending when …, It is full of humorous moments.
F: It's expertly directed by …, It stars … as …, There are exceptional / mediocre performances from …, It had the audience laughing, It's a must-see.
B: It's beautifully / terribly written by …, The images will stay long in the reader's mind, I couldn't put it down, It's well-worth reading, If you only read one book this year, make sure it's ….

7   **Sample answer**

The novel *Atonement* by Ian McEwan, set in Britain in the 1930s and during the Second World War, has been made into a very successful film starring Keira Knightley and James McAvoy.

The novel tells the story of a thirteen-year-old girl with a very vivid imagination who wrongly accuses the servant's son, Robbie, of a crime. The novel is very well-written but I found the beginning slow-moving. In fact, I didn't think I would be able to finish it. However, the descriptions of the Second World War in the second part of the book are very emotional and well-worth reading.

The film is more fast-moving than the novel, and is better because of this. The performances of McAvoy and Knightley are exceptional, and are one of the main reasons this film is so good. There is an incredible scene of Dunkirk beach in France during the war, which contains thousands of extras.

I definitely recommend both the book and the film, but I prefer the film. I couldn't stop thinking about it after I had seen it. If you only watch one film this year, make sure it's *Atonement*.

First-rate food (pages 38–39)

2a   In this context, 'OK' means satisfactory, but not particularly good.

2b   ☆☆☆☆☆ **Fantastic!:** excellent, amazing, exceptional, first-rate, memorable, out of this world, stunning, tasty
☆☆☆☆ **Good:** acceptable, not bad, reasonable, satisfactory
☆☆ **OK:** dull, forgettable, nothing special, so-so
☆ **Horrible:** awful, disgusting, dreadful, horrid, shocking, terrible

3   **b)** not bad, nothing special, out of this world, so-so

4   Write a review about a café or restaurant which serves food from a particular country or culture. Describe the quality of the food and the atmosphere. Say how it is typical of food from the country and whether you recommend it.

The best reviews will be included on our website.

6   **Sample answer**

I am a Mexican student studying in Cardiff, Wales, and imagine my surprise when I found a branch of the Mexican restaurant chain Wahaca in the city centre!

The first thing you notice about Wahaca is the amazing atmosphere. Even though there were lots of people, it didn't feel too cramped. There were colourful murals on the wall and lots of pot plants, which gave it a natural feel. I can tell you the music was typical and

it definitely made me feel at home! The staff were friendly, but they were very busy, and didn't have much time to chat. That's not like the waiters back in Mexico!

Wahaca's menu is more Mexican-style than authentic Mexican food. Many of the dishes contain ingredients that you don't find on menus in Mexico, like tacitos made with European feta cheese. They tasted OK, but were instantly forgettable. However, the pork pibil tacos were stunning. I had to order some more!

I would definitely recommend Wahaca – for some tasty food and a real feel of Mexico!

Gamer or n00b? (pages 40–41)

1b   **bug:** an error in game's programming or design

MMO (Massively Multiplayer Online): Similar to a Role Playing Game with a huge online world of bots and human players.

Easter eggs: hidden features such as a new character or secret level

expansion: an addition to an existing game. These add-ons include new game areas, weapons and objects and an extended storyline.

f2p (Free-to-play): used for video games where players can access a large portion of the content without paying

fan-base: The fans of a particular person, team, film, etc.

First-Person Shooter (FPS): A shooting game seen through the playable character's eyes.

gameplay: everything to do with how you play a game, e.g. the player's interaction with the character, rules, challenges, storyline.

graphics: the images, characters and locations in a game

level cap: the maximum level a player can reach in a game

n00b or newbie: a new and unskilled player of a game

RPG (Role Playing Game): A game in which a role is played by the gamer, who makes choices and decides on actions.

2   **a)** False   **b)** False   **c)** True   **d)** True   **e)** False   **f)** False   **g)** True

4   **Sample answer**

Destiny, released by Bungie and Activision, was a much-hyped video game, but it has failed to live up to expectations.

Players take on the role of a Guardian, the defender of Earth's last safe city. They travel to different planets to destroy alien threats. The game is a first-person shooter which includes a few elements of MMO, for example players can only communicate with some of the other players in the game.

Sadly, I found the game disappointing. Despite having the whole universe there, the planets are broken down into small zones. The story is not very engaging and there's a lot of repetitive gameplay. I visited the same areas several times. The only person you speak to is your Ghost, and he sounded bored.

Let's look at the positives. Since its release, Bungie have brought out several expansions and the battles and locations are getting better. If Bungie wants players to keep coming back, then it needs more new locations, enemies and weapons.

Has *Destiny* lived up to the hype? No, it hasn't, but if it continues to get better, maybe I'll give it another try.

Don't miss it! (pages 42–43)

2   The following are mentioned: visitor numbers, site or building, ticket policy, merchandise, enjoyment

3

(+) the plus points	(–) the disappointments	Suggestions / recommendations
Beautiful artwork Visitors left with huge smiles	Visitor numbers	run one- or two-picture exhibitions lower ticket prices operate a queuing system

4   could try (one- or two-picture exhibitions), could look at (lowering the entry fee to as little as £1), might want (to operate a queuing system)

7   **Sample answer**

This summer I visited Sea Life Adventure at Southend-on-Sea in the UK. I really enjoyed my visit, although there were a few things the aquarium could do to improve the visitor experience.

The aquarium is independently-run and this gave the whole centre a more personal feel. Regular talks on the marine life were interesting and given by the young staff. They were all very friendly, although some were more informative than others. It made a change to see species that you can find in the local River Thames.

Running an aquarium is clearly an expensive business. The ticket was not cheap and the staff tried very hard to sell me a season ticket. If the aquarium wants to raise some funds, it could try selling better merchandise. The gift shop had very little in it. They might also need to reconsider the café menu which was limited and expensive.

All in all, this was a fun experience, but I would think twice about paying the entrance fee for another visit.

Songs on a playlist (pa5.5

2   **Suggested answers**

a) 6 **b)** 2 **c)** 1 **d)** 3 **e)** 2 **f)** 1 **g)** 3 **h)** 6 **i)** 4 **j)** 5 **k)** 6 **l)** 5 **m)** 4 **n)** 3

4   **Sample answer**

Anyone who has heard Paloma Faith's music knows she can sing. But can she reproduce those performances live?

I was lucky enough to get tickets for Paloma's concert in Thetford Forest, Norfolk. Dressed in sparkling black and silver, Paloma's look was as stunning as her voice. There were over five thousand people at the outdoor venue. Some had even brought picnics and chairs, but they were soon on their feet and dancing to the soul hits. They really loved it and so did I.

For me, the highlights of the evening were the beautiful 'Do you want the truth or something beautiful?' and 'New York', probably her best-known song and one which always reminds me of the summer. On this warm evening, with the lights in the trees around the stage, the venue was the perfect setting for a summer concert.

Can Paloma Faith sing live? You bet! And five thousand people would agree with me.

'I'm so fed up!' (page 45)

1   *sorry* can be used in all of these sentences.
a) *I'm sorry* is used here as an apology.
b) *Be / Feel sorry for someone* shows that the speaker has sympathy for someone who is in a bad situation.
c) *I'm sorry* in this context means the speaker feels sad or disappointed.
d) *Sorry?* is used when you have not heard what someone has said and you want them to repeat it.
e) *Sorry to bother you* is a formal phrase used in a similar way to *Excuse me*.

2   **1** c **2** a **3** d **4** a **5** b **6** c **7** e **8** d

3   **a)** I'm really sorry to hear about what happened.

b) Please accept my apologies for … / I would very much like to come.

c) Unfortunately, I have another meeting on that day. / Please accept my apologies for being unable to attend. / I would be delighted to attend and look forward to meeting with you.

d) Thanks, that would be great.

4   As you know, I usually go running every day, but I had an accident last week. I had a very bad fall and I am walking with a stick right now. I'm getting about OK, but the doctor has said that I can't do any sport for three months. I'm so fed up!

I'll be in your area next week. Have you got any suggestions of things I could do? Now that I think of it, why don't you come too?

Sample answer

Dear Sophie

Sorry not to be in touch before, I've been so busy!

I'm really sorry to hear about the accident. I'm not surprised that you're fed up – you are always so active! You must tell me what happened.

So pleased you are coming next week. I'd love to meet up. What day will you be here? I work until 5.30 but I'm free at the weekend, of course.

There's lots we can do. There's a great photo exhibition on at the Town Hall. A friend of mine went to see it last week and he said it was great! But if you don't want to be on your feet, we could go and see a film instead. There's always a good choice of films at our local cinema. And why don't we go for a coffee after? My favourite place is The China Teacup. Their coffee is the best and they have really scrummy cakes.

Let me know what you fancy doing. And don't worry, we can still have fun!

See you next week!

Love,

Trish

Volunteering (pages 46–47)

2   Sample answers

a) Why do you want to volunteer for this charity?
b) How much do you know about what this charity does?
c) How much time will you be able to volunteer each week?
d) What are your interests?
e) Do you have any special skills?
f) How can you get here?

3   Sample answers

a) We expect you to show the same kind of commitment you would in any job: arrive on time, complete all your hours and be kind and respectful to colleagues and the people you are helping.

b) Volunteering can help you cope with personal sadness or frustration at world issues. You can support a cause even if you don't have money to spare. You will learn new skills such as organising, time management and teamwork. It can also help you to get an idea of future paid work and whether you would be suited to it. Volunteering can give you confidence and a sense of pride. Many people volunteer because it stops them getting bored or just because they enjoy it!

c) It is better to give some time than to give none at all. Even if you can only give a couple of hours, that will help. But we do ask that you volunteer at the same time each week or month.

4   a) advice

6   Sample answer

Hi Noah

Good to hear from you. I think volunteering is a fantastic idea. I spend one day a week helping out at a sports club and I love it! It's a great way to meet people and looking after the children has really helped my confidence.

It would be a good idea if you made a list of your interests and skills. I know you like playing the guitar. Have you thought about helping out at the youth orchestra?

It might help to look up some charities you are interested in and see if they have a local group. If I were you, I'd do a search on localvolunteer.com. I think you should check out the college noticeboard too. There are always adverts on there. When you find one you're interested in, email or ring. Let them know how many hours you can work. Don't forget to ask them if they provide transport because you can't drive, can you? Then you can arrange to visit them to see if you like working there.

Hope this helps! Good luck!

Toni

'Where should I stay?' (pages 48–49)

4   Sample answers

Hi Susanna

Of course I remember your aunt and uncle. We met at your sister's wedding.

I'm glad to hear you are bringing them here. I'm sure they'll love it. I remember your aunt told me that they enjoyed going for long walks. How about walking along the shore path? There's a six-mile walk which starts at South Queensferry and there are lots of interesting places along the way. I can recommend the ice creams at Dalmeny House or perhaps they could stop for tea at the café in Cramond village.

As far as hotels go, one option is 94 DR. It's a bit of a walk from the town centre, but it's perfect for a weekend away. The breakfast is amazing! It might be a bit on the expensive side, so why don't you send them the weblink and see what they think? I suggest checking if they have any rooms available though, because I know they sometimes get booked up quickly.

Let me know when you are arriving, it would be great to meet up!

Speak soon,

Hi Laura

Thanks for your email. Good to hear you're going to be here next week. Where is the IT training course? I guess you'll need a hotel somewhere near. You can't go far wrong with Cityroomz. It's in a central location and the rooms are modern and fun. It's not too expensive either, so that'll please your boss.

Perhaps you could consider taking your new colleagues to Stockbridge? It's only a ten-minute walk from Princes Street and it's well-worth a visit. It has some lovely streets and squares and there are a lot of unusual shops and galleries. It's a great place to eat too. If the weather is bad, why don't you take them to a museum? There are lots in Edinburgh. My favourite is The National Museum of Scotland. There's something for everyone there! And make sure you spend some time in the roof garden. Not many people know about it, but you get a great view of the city from up there.

Hope this helps and enjoy yourselves!

Regards,

Hi there, Mo!

Great to hear from you! Your cousin sounds fun. She's going to love Edinburgh! And you're lucky – you're arriving during the Fringe festival! I suggest going to the half-price ticket place on the Mound and seeing what shows are on. Or why not take her to the Scottish National Gallery of Modern Art? It's a great place to spend a few hours and even better, it's free to get in! You might have to pay to see special exhibitions. Perhaps you could check out their website.

I can recommend the youth hostel on Haddington Place. It's not a typical youth hostel – it feels more like a hotel. If your cousin likes going out, she might find the area a bit quiet at night, so you could think about Cityroomz instead. Cityroomz is in a more central location. It's more expensive, but the price includes breakfast.

I'm going to be away next week so I'll probably miss you. It's a real shame. But tell me all about it and I'm sure we'll get together again soon.

Have a great time!

Love,

What sort of camper are you? (pages 50–51)

2 *really* goes in front of an adjective: *a really great time, really tired, really unhappy, really good fun, really excited*

loads of means the same *as lots of* and is very colloquial: *loads of cookies, loads of mosquito repellent*

so has a similar meaning to *very*, and is used to give extra emphasis: *so tired, so unhappy, so excited*. It is not used after an article: ~~a so great time~~

Anyway, is used to change the subject or return to a previous subject: *Anyway, we all had chocolate biscuits. Anyway,* can also be used to signal that you are ending your message. *Anyway, how are things with you?*

A bit means the same as *a little*. It is informal and can sometimes be used in an ironic sense, i.e. it actually means 'a lot': *a bit tired, a bit unhappy, a bit excited*

Awesome! Is an exclamation to show how much you like something, e.g. *We're having a great time here at the campsite. Awesome! We all had chocolate biscuits and popcorn for breakfast this morning. Awesome!*

Now we're off to the beach. Awesome!

3 **a)** Yes, Kai and George are friends.
b) It is informal and friendly.
c) They make it more informal.

5 **a)** doesn't know
b) likely
c) pleasant
d) semi-formal

6 **Sample answer**

Dear Melanie

I'm writing because I saw your advert for a log cabin in a recent issue of 'Speak English!' magazine.

I'm a student from Japan and I've been studying in Liverpool for a couple of months. My parents are coming to visit me in the summer and I'm looking for somewhere where we can all stay for two weeks. Your log cabin looks ideal! My father is a keen birdwatcher and I'm sure he would love to stay in a forest.

Please could you let me know if the log cabin is available for the first two weeks of July? And how much would it cost for three people to stay there? Is it easy to reach or would we require our own transport? Also, can you tell me if there are any wildlife reserves nearby?

I look forward to hearing from you.

Best wishes

Azusa

I look forward to your reply (pages 52–53)

1 The style of the reply is not appropriate because it is too informal.

2 The correct order is: f, e, h, d, b, c, a, g

3 **a)** It won't be necessary to **b)** received, goods **c)** making good progress **d)** accept **e)** arrange **f)** your request **g)** her actions **h)** a large number of **i)** further details

4 **a)** True **b)** True **c)** False. Phrases using 'get' are often used in informal emails. **d)** False. Sentences in formal emails tend to be longer. **e)** False. Informal language used in a formal email does not give a good impression. **f)** True **g)** Exclamation marks are often used in informal emails. **h)** True

5 **Sample answer**

Dear Tomiko

I am writing to thank you for your very kind invitation. It was such a pleasant surprise.

I would be very happy to accept your invitation to the conference and to attend your presentation.

I was wondering if you could send me some more details about the location of the conference and suitable accommodation in the city.

I would be grateful if I could bring my colleague Lena with me. She is a very experienced member of the personnel team and would welcome the opportunity to meet with colleagues from the Tokyo office.

As it is quite an early start on 4 April, would it be possible for myself and Lena to arrive on the previous day? Simon Todd is responsible for making travel arrangements. Please would you contact him on stodd@businesswise.co.uk

I am very much looking forward to meeting you and to finding out more about Tokyo and Japan.

Yours sincerely,

Yours sincerely (pages 54–55)

1 food service, customer relations, horticulture and security

3 Ethan follows all of the guidelines except for the first one: using a neutral email address. The email address that Ethan uses could give the impression that he is not being serious in this situation.

4a Yours sincerely Ethan could also use *Yours faithfully, Yours* and *I look forward to hearing from you.*

4b The most informal phrases are *Love, Lots of love* and *Let me know.*

5 In a formal email, Ethan could use *Dear Mr Reed, Dear Sir, Dear Madam, Dear Sir/Madam.*

The most informal phrases are *Hi Joe, Hello there* and *Hi guys.*

6 **Possible answers**

In a formal letter you don't have an email address or subject header. You will need to supply your contact details and write the date. Your contact details and the date are written in the top right-hand corner. Sometimes the writer will also write the address of the person they are writing to on the left. If the letter is handwritten rather than typed, then neat handwriting will give a good impression!

7 **Sample answer**

Dear Sir / Madam

I am writing in reply to your advertisement for vacancies which I saw on the noticeboard at English Plus Language School where I am a student.

I am twenty years old and I am a maths student. I am a keen swimmer and am currently attending a lifeguard training course once a week. We are learning skills such as making quick decisions and working as part of a team. I would like the opportunity to learn more about working as a lifeguard. For this reason, I would be interested in your vacancies in water safety.

I would be grateful if you could tell me how many hours a week you need people to work. Also, is this is a seasonal vacancy or for the whole year? I am aware that Diamond Springs has a number of amusement parks. Please could you also tell me where the vacancies are based.

I look forward to hearing from you.

Yours sincerely,

In character (pages 56–57)

4 **Sample notes**

Character
Lena: wiry, nervous, plays with her hair, has something on her mind, late 20s, dark-skinned, speaks excitedly
Ending
'You must be Lena,' the man said.
Storyline
- text message from Paul, a friend of her father. He's going to be late.
- rushes into the hotel foyer, kind but busy
- accompanies her across the city in a tram
- fall quiet, thinks back over what her mother had told her about her father, arguments, he had left, she was only two
- get to a small house in an ordinary street
- door opens, tall, wiry nervous man

5 **Sample answer**

Lena walked into the hotel and looked around anxiously. It was early afternoon and the hotel was quiet. A loud beep broke the silence. It was a text message from Paul, a friend of her father's. 'Running late,' the message said. 'Be there in ten.'

Lena found it hard to stand still. She had waited a long time for today and she was excited and nervous. Finally Paul hurried up to her and they walked quickly down to the tram stop.

The tram was busy, and as it swayed through the streets, the pair fell quiet and Lena thought about what her mother had told her about her father – about his passion for football, his busy job, the arguments, the door which had slammed behind him one day when Lena was only two.

Paul took Lena down an ordinary-looking street to a small terraced house. Suddenly she wished she had not come. What if her father was angry? Paul knocked firmly on the door and a tall man came to the door. He looked nervously past Paul.

'You must be Lena,' he said.

A discovery and a map (page 58)

1b detached, dusty, high-rise, isolated, neglected, ordinary, ruined, run-down, shabby, terraced, typical, well-situated

3 **Sample notes**

Where is the house?
in my local town, residential road,
Make notes to describe the house.
Victorian, run-down, overgrown garden, back from the road

How does Evan feel in the house?
frustrated: a lot to be done

Why is Evan there?
Has inherited it from an aunt he did not know very well

What discovery does Evan make?
a small shed at the bottom of the garden, door hanging off

Why does Evan have a map?
He finds it in a chest in the shed, map of a street, X marked on it

How does the story end?
Evan realised with a shock that the map was of the street where his parents still lived. X marked the spot of the old oak tree in the garden.

4 **Sample answer**

The house was not as Evan had imagined. His elderly aunt had not been wealthy and when the solicitor told him he'd inherited her property, Evan had thought it would be a shabby flat in a poor part of town. The house was neglected, but it must have been pretty once. Evan sighed

as he stood in the kitchen on that autumn day. There was so much to do.

Evan wandered into the garden. He could make out a dark shape at the end of the garden and he made his way towards it. It was an old shed, the door hanging off. Climbing over the door, Evan found a large wooden chest. He swept the dust off the top and it opened with a creak. There was a map inside. It showed a street with a few houses on it. One of the houses was marked with a large X.

Evan peered more closely and realised with a shock that the map was of Tyler Street, where his parents still lived. The X marked the spot where the oak tree stood.

Recommending a book (page 59)

2 **a)** villain **b)** theme **c)** setting **d)** cliffhanger **e)** relationship **f)** plot

3 **1** g **2** a **3** f **4** d **5** c **6** i **7** b **8** e **9** h

An unexpected ending (page 59)

6 **Sample answer**

Hi Tara

Thanks for your email. You said you wanted to read a book with interesting characters. I can definitely recommend *Frankenstein*, written by Mary Shelley.

Everyone knows the monster in Frankenstein, but the original story is well-worth reading. The monster is very ugly, so everyone is horrible to him. Is he evil? Or is it just because of the way he is treated?

The monster was created by Victor Frankenstein. Victor learns the secret of life while studying at university. He creates the monster from old body parts from the graveyard, some strange chemicals and a mysterious spark. Some people say this is electricity.

The relationship between Victor and the monster is very complicated. Victor's monster kills Victor's brother and Victor feels guilty about his creation. Victor changes a lot during the novel. He starts out as an innocent youth who loves science and he ends as a guilty and broken man. However, he and the monster that he created are both memorable characters.

Make sure you read *Frankenstein* and let me know what you think of it!

Write back soon,

Practice test 1: Part 1 (page 60)

1 **Sample answer**

These days students have plenty of choice in their studies. There are many courses available and different ways to study too. However, on the downside, deciding on a course can be difficult.

An increasing number of people are choosing to study online. One reason for this is that they have no transport costs and can study from home. In addition, it is a far better option for people who work part-time. Although it is convenient to study at home, it can be difficult to ignore social media and household chores.

The majority of students still choose to go to college. They have regular classes and homework tasks and, in my opinion, this makes it easier for them to organise their studies. It is also a good way to meet other students with similar interests and gives them the opportunity to discuss their ideas. For subjects like science, the facilities of a college are essential.

As far as I am concerned, the advantages of going to college outweigh the reasons for studying online. However, it is very good that colleges offer online courses for those who need them.

Practice test 1: Part 2 (page 61)

2   Sample answer (Article)

Hurricanes in the USA, drought in Australia, floods in the Philippines – the effects of climate change are always in the news. But what can we do that will make any difference?

World leaders meet regularly to discuss climate change. They need to. The pollution caused by factories and traffic is a major factor in global warming. We need worldwide agreement on issues like these and we need it fast.

Do you think there's nothing you can do? Think again. Slowing down climate change can only happen with a change in attitude. Just imagine. If we all turned down our heating by one degree Celsius, it would have an immediate effect on the electricity we use each day. Recycle your clothes instead of putting them in the bin and you're cutting down on waste that goes to landfill. What's more, it's so easy to do.

Don't rely on politicians and businesspeople to change things. Set them a good example first. Who can save the planet? You can!

3   Sample answer (Email)

Dear Mr Hunting

Thank you for your email. It was good to hear from you. I am really pleased to hear that you are thinking of starting up a running club.

There are not many sports facilities in this area so I think people would definitely be interested. A lot of people commute to work from here and get home quite late. For this reason, I think you should only ask people to come once a week or at the weekends.

Have you thought of handing out leaflets at the train station? It would be a good way to advertise and then you could chat to people about their sports interests. Perhaps you could consider running a football club too? My friends and I play at the park on Saturdays. We love football, but we're not very good! It would be great to have some training at the weekends.

Let me know if you start the running club and I'll give it a try.

Best wishes,

4   Sample answer (Report)

Introduction

The purpose of this report is to evaluate possible solutions to traffic congestion in my area. Over recent years people have begun to move from the city to live in nearby towns in order to avoid the effects of pollution. Unfortunately this has increased the number of rush hour commuters.

Park and ride schemes

Park and ride schemes allow people to park outside the city and ride on a free bus into the centre. The scheme is often popular with the elderly and shoppers but is not used much by regular commuters.

Cycle lanes

Building cycle lanes next to existing roads encourages people to cycle instead of drive to work. However, the building work is expensive and not all roads in the city centre are suitable.

Congestion charging

In this scheme, people are charged for driving into the centre at busy times. The scheme is often unpopular with residents at first but has been successful in larger cities like London.

Recommendations

In general, congestion charging has been the most successful of the above solutions. I would therefore recommend that we consider a similar scheme in our city.

Practice test 2: Part 1 (page 62)

1   Sample answer

There is plenty of information available today about the benefits of a balanced diet. Yet today's teenagers eat an increasingly unhealthy diet. But are teenagers at fault or are we all to blame?

The media is full of advertising for unhealthy foods such as sweets and chocolate, and fast food restaurants. Even so-called healthy options, like breakfast cereals, are full of sugar. How can we expect teenagers not to eat these when they are constantly faced with images of them?

More could be done by schools to educate their pupils about a healthy diet. Schools teach students about healthy eating but very often school canteens serve food which is cheap but not nutritious. In this way, schools are encouraging bad habits among teenagers.

Unhealthy food is often the cheapest food in the shops. Teenagers who would rather spend their money on other things are more likely to buy food which is cheap but lacks nutritional value.

In conclusion, teenagers should take responsibility for their own health. But they need to be set a good example. Society and the media could do much more to help them.

Practice test 2: Part 2 (page 63)

2   Sample answer (Email)

Hi Rajeev

Many thanks for your email. Sorry I've not been in touch. I've been very busy studying for my exams.

Your project sounds interesting. I go to the computer programming club after school on Tuesdays. It's awesome. One of the teachers runs it and she knows everything about computers so I can ask her for lots of advice.

Last term I also went to geography club. I went with a friend of mine who's really into geography. But it wasn't my thing. People used the time to do their geography homework. That was a great idea because there were lots of books and magazines to help them. But I'd rather use my free time for something else!

If you want to get the most out of a club, you should go regularly, so make sure it's something you're really interested in. The best thing about clubs is meeting other people with the same interests. At the computer programming club, I've got to know kids from different years who all like the same things as me.

Let me know how your project goes!

Love,

3   Sample answer (Review)

It's no surprise that my favourite device is my iPad. Once you've owned one of these, you'll never look at another tablet.

One reason I love my iPad is that it's thin and light. It means I can watch a movie wherever I want. And it's awesome when my friends come round and we can pass it round easily. The screen is really clear. I really like reading books on it, so my mum's happy too. The battery lasts a lot longer than the battery on a laptop.

And of course, the iPad looks really cool. It also has Touch ID which scans your fingerprint so it knows who you are. I think that's my favourite feature!

For me, the only negative is that it's a bit expensive. I won mine in a competition, but now I can't imagine life without it. Get yourself a Saturday job so you can afford one.

No teenager should be without an iPad. It's fun to use with your friends and you'll even enjoy reading your school textbooks on it!

4   Sample answer (Story)

From the moment Kerry woke up, she knew it was going to be a different kind of day. The sun was shining after days of dull rainy mornings.

As Kerry was drinking her morning coffee, she looked out of the window at her Dad's dirty old car and something caught her eye. In the mud on the back someone had written: Kerry – call me. 07756 628028.

Kerry stared at the message. Who had written it? Was it a friend? Someone playing a joke? Or was it someone in trouble?

With trembling fingers, Kerry rang the number. A woman's voice answered.

'Hi,' Kerry said hesitantly. 'You left your number.'

'Is that Kerry?' the voice replied. 'I found your bag in the street. It had your name and address but not what flat you live in. I'm at work, but you can come and collect it.'

Kerry looked at the hook on the door where she usually hung her schoolbag. It was empty.

'Where do you work?' asked Kerry.

'I'm at the Theatre Royal,' the woman said. 'I'm an actress. You might have seen me on TV.'

'TV?' said Kerry. What a surprise!

5   Sample answer (Set text)

Macbeth by William Shakespeare is set in Scotland and is about an ambitious soldier, called Macbeth. In the story there is one event which changes Macbeth's life forever, and that is the murder of King Duncan. Three witches predict that Macbeth will one day be crowned King of Scotland. Macbeth's wife, Lady Macbeth, is also very ambitious. She is a strong woman and she persuades Macbeth to kill Duncan so that he can be King immediately.

At the start of the story, Macbeth is a brave general who earns his soldiers' respect, but after the murder everything changes. Macbeth becomes King, but the murder of Duncan leads to other murders. Macbeth becomes angry and insecure and his soldiers start to lose their respect for him. In the final battle, Macbeth is no longer a good general and he is easily beaten by the army of Duncan's son. Macbeth is killed and there is peace in the kingdom again. The story of Macbeth is about the dangers of ambition and corruption and this is symbolised by Duncan's murder.

Material written by: Fiona Davis

Publisher: Jacquie Bloese

Development Editor: Sarah Silver

FCE Consultant: Lynda Edwards

Designer: Andrea Lewis

Cover Design: Eddie Rego

Picture Research: Amparo Escobedo

Picture credits:
Great work: U. Schanker, D Paul Morris, Hulton Archive, P M Tacca, VI Images, J Kobal Foundation/Getty Images
Transport going forward: J. Sullivan, H. Laubel/ iStockphoto; Wikimedia Commons
A meat-free future: annebaek, m-imagephotography, J. Greig, zuzusaturn, Aifos/iStockphoto
Too young for Facebook?: Slonov, R-i-s-e, ulimi, lilu330, subarashii21/iStockphoto
Digital generation: Vasiliki Varvaki, isitsharp, N. McComber, T. Fullum, DRB Images, LLC/iStockphoto
Criminal activity: I. McDonnell/iStockphoto
Celebrity status: Yuri, Brosa, E. Querini, Nikkolia, fotografixx, carlacdesign, kowalska-art/iStockphoto
Taking a gap year: MShep2, N. McComber, si_arts, M. Zarya, OcusFocus/iStockphoto
'Why here? Why now?': andresr, MJTH, PeopleImages/ iStockphoto
Take sleep seriously!: PeopleImages, Squaredpixels/ iStockphoto
Hallowe'en: A time to have fun: Vlue/Shutterstock; pablocalvog, mediaphotos/iStockphoto
Never give up!: aluxum, J. Horrocks/iStockphoto
Learning something new: mantosh/iStockphoto
A vibrant city: serdjophoto, kelvinjay, BillPhilpot/ iStockphoto; A. Wallace/Shutterstock
An eco-friendly home: Mark Watkinson/Beehive illustration; M. Rall/Getty Images
The next best thing: Paul Moran/Beehive illustration; KatarzynaBialasiewicz, MichaelDeLeon/iStockphoto
A must-see film: FoxSearch/Everett, Moviestore/REX; Buyenlarge, A. Edwards, C. Eshelman/Getty images
First-rate food: eli_asenova, A-Digit /iStockphoto
Gamer or n00b?: Cheng Chi Lin/iStockphoto; O. Berg/ AFP/Getty Images

'Don't miss it!': L. Neal/AFP, Archive Photos/Getty Images
Songs on a playlist: RoBeDeRo/iStockphoto
'I'm so fed up': LittleBee80/iStockphoto
Volunteering: beakraus, philsajonesen, N. McComber, artishokcs/iStockphoto
'Where should I stay?': 94DR Guest House; Edinburgh Central Youth Hostel; K. Bialasiewicz/iStockphoto
What sort of camper are you? K. Bell, davemantel/ iStockphoto; F. Tanneau/AFP/Getty Images
'I look forward to your reply': DragonImages/ iStockphoto
'Yours sincerely': tropicalpixsingapore, LifesizeImages, A Di Noia, C B Photography Inc, Viorika/iStockphoto
In character: krechet/iStockphoto
A discovery and a map: Gerrit_de_Vries, macroworld/ iStockphoto; J. McIlroy/Shutterstock

Printed in the UK by Bell & Bain Ltd, Glasgow

FSC
www.fsc.org

MIX
Paper from
responsible sources
FSC® C007785